T0129843

How Did I Fund My Startup?

STORIES FROM ACROSS THE GLOBE INCLUDING
SILICON VALLEY USING INNOVATIVE FUNDING MEANS

Inspiring Stories of Funding by Dynamic
Entrepreneurs from USA, UK, India and Singapore.

Mehul Darooka

authorHOUSE®

AuthorHouse™
1663 Liberty Drive
Bloomington, IN 47403
www.authorhouse.com
Phone: 1 (800) 839-8640

Published by AuthorHouse 03/20/2019

ISBN: 978-1-5462-7399-8 (sc)
ISBN: 978-1-5462-7412-4 (e)

Print information available on the last page.

Any people depicted in stock imagery provided by Getty Images are models, and such images are being used for illustrative purposes only. Certain stock imagery © Getty Images.

This book is printed on acid-free paper.

Because of the dynamic nature of the Internet, any web addresses or links contained in this book may have changed since publication and may no longer be valid. The views expressed in this work are solely those of the author and do not necessarily reflect the views of the publisher, and the publisher hereby disclaims any responsibility for them.

Contents

Foreword

Amongst the various words and terms that will go down in history to denote ideas that changed the world, Startups will be way up there. For if there is anything that is a most tangible reflection of following one's dreams, listening to one's instincts and trusting that inner voice- it's a startup. Entrepreneurship is not just about an idea, it's also as much about having confidence and conviction in that idea. Once that is in place and, you find what makes it work, then is perhaps not so much to do with the uniqueness of the idea, as it is to do with the drive with which it is pursued.

It is precisely this that I found stands out in every one of the success stories so ably, lucidly and concisely put together by Mehul Darooka in the book you hold in your hands. For while this book may delve into the more pragmatic aspect of innovative funding, it also very subtly underlines a basic truth of life-that if you can dream it, you can do it.

How else do you explain the fact that in a scenario where funding for startups is perceived as the biggest challenge/obstacle for any new venture, as many as 20 plus different strategies worked? How is that each person had a completely varied, novel and, in some cases, even bizarre way of getting together the economics to drive his or her idea and yet each one's effort hit the bull's eye? The simple explanation is that while each took a different route, the starting and finishing points were the same. All started with an unflinching belief in their ideas and all were headed towards one goal - to make it a reality.

So while some approached Venture Capitalists or Angel Investors and others reached out to family, friends or even former or current employers for funding, each was finally able to convince the person or party across the table mainly because of the passion and confidence they exuded.

Having said that, the importance of hard work and the value of thinking a project through in detail cannot be underestimated. And this is precisely where this book, I feel, plays an indispensable part in a way that none other I have come across does. It lays down for entrepreneurs the very important structure that their ideas need to follow to enable them to take flight and arrive at their logical conclusions. Significantly, it also conveys the timeline for each route taken, along with the pros and cons entailed. In a nutshell, what it does for entrepreneurs is to minimize confusion, maximize clarity and materialize concretely the road ahead.

Going through the stories of each of the entrepreneurs profiled in the book, what also struck me was the sheer range of the startups. From healthy eating to quirky products to bargain solutions to anti-virus software, the products conceived, devised and developed span a wide canvas. While some are completely new to the market, others have taken on competition from already existing similar, products which they have managed to counter simply by making theirs a better and more user-friendly version. This again brings home yet another tried and tested rule (is this beginning to sound like a lesson on life skills? If so, just as well too!) that however crowded the market place, there is always room for quality. This is also precisely why in a market overcrowded with books on Entrepreneurship, you will soon see why this one flies off the shelves with such ease.

Finally, I would like to point out that while at the outset this book may seem like a perfect guide for those wanting to get into startups and looking for viable ways of funding, it's as much a treasured read for investors wanting to put in their money into sound ventures, for it enables one to get a detailed insight into what works and what doesn't in the market. Too often one tends to reject ideas that look untenable and hence un-fundable and then, much to the anguish of those who first rejected it, they turn out to be veritable block busters! Haven't we all heard of Facebook rejecting WhatsApp co-founder Brian Acton for a job and then paying $19 billion to buy what could have been its own home-grown product?

So, while on one end, this book will give its young readers some invaluable guidance on how to find, fund and further their ideas, at the other, it will also provide seasoned investors with possibly more wisdom before they decide on the next venture they are looking to place their bet and money on. Could there be a better win-win situation for all concerned?

Sunanda Mehta
(Former Resident Editor, The Indian Express, A leading English daily of India)

Acknowledgements

It's not easy to dedicatedly work on a concept and on something close to your heart if your surroundings are not supportive. Those who matter to you and to whom you matter will always strive for your success. They cherish your thoughts and add zeal to your task. Therefore, I did never lose a chance of thanking those who have made a difference for me and have helped me achieve this second book of mine. After my first 3 successful books, the second being in 3 editions, I am glad and honored to present this next book to my readers. Therefore, it is needless to say I must thank some of them who have made this possible. First and foremost, I would like to thank my lovely parents, because of whom I am here. They have instilled in me immense love, respect and care and determination, willpower and most importantly the need to be a good human. Next on my radar comes my lovely wife Arpita, who has been my strength and my biggest critic as well. She has always helped me and supported me come what may. She is my lifeline, my happiness and my love. Finally, from my lovely family's side, my mathematics professor sister based out of USA, who has always ensured I don't lose track and am ably supported by all. She is, she was and she will be the most admired daughter and sister for us.

Of course, needless to say, I am indebted to the Almighty for making me what I am today and trust he will always take care of us. When I was in between this book, my mother encountered a deadly disease, which, by the grace of god, is very much under control and I am really indebted to that superpower to take care of my mom. I have a similar book published in India and am thankful to my publishers in India for their trust in me. It's in 3rd edition now with 2 in English and one in regional language of India. A big thanks to all my storytellers to be kind enough to patiently answer my questions, get interviewed by me and give in all their support to make this a success. Not to forget my partners in crime, M/s SME Join up for coming out with this concept. Last but not the least, my love and thanks to all my family, friends and relatives who always believed in me!

-**Mehul Darooka**

Introduction

Funding! A core to any business, backbone to any growth and necessary ingredient for any development!

Startups in India have typically been bootstrapped with little or no funds up-front. Infosys, Reliance - the dream is endless, the funds limited. Traditionally entrepreneurs/businessmen opted for financing from banks and financial institutions. But with more and more startups having only digital capital, traditional funds have dried up. Today the lender has nothing more than a PowerPoint, may be a website and two young freshers from college to mortgage for the funds he gives.

But the entrepreneur has risen to even this challenge. They have spurned these traditional methods and figured out innovative ways to fund their ventures.

In this book, we peep into some such stories. Some of the entrepreneurs are known names like Mr. Kailash Katkar, owner of Quick Heal-India's leading Anti-Virus Manufacturing company or Mrs. Shubra Chaddha, owner of Chumbak-India's leading gifting and personalization company or Mr. Siddhartha M Jain, Executive Producer of the movie Ragini MMS. Some are lesser known like Rajesh of Programmer and Samir from Mobikon. But they all have used innovative, maybe crazy, ways to fund their startups.

However, this book is not biographies of these great entrepreneurs. This is a book dedicated to helping you find innovative and alternative ways to fund your startup. The book examines each of these methods and lays bare the pros and cons of each method.

- Each of the methods is explained by a startup/company who has already used that method for funding

- Each of the stories carries the journey of the startup, how they used the method and what were the implications

- The Author, who is also an investor, critically analyses each method, its pros and cons, should you attempt to try out these methods.

- There is a FUND-O-METER at the end of each story to help you judge the merits of this approach.

Mrs. Sunanda Mehta, Resident Editor, Indian Express, Pune has been kind enough to give us a Foreword for the book and has emphasized the importance of such platforms to educate entrepreneurs to know about the nuances of funding.

1

IRock India

 Irock India was a Bollywood film development and production company. IRock believed in genre-specific, 'high-concept films'. Their claim to fame was RAGINI MMS, which was acquired by Balaji Telefilms (a leading Film Production company of India). LAST YEAR iRock produced youth-centric DISCO VALLEY with Viacom18 and a cause-driven FILM KILL THE RAPIST. Both these films released in 2014.

Former Founder: Siddhartha M Jain

 Siddharth Jain is a movie crazy Bollywood-bug-bitten entrepreneur who wants to create high concept movies with strong youth focus. He started his career from Hollywood where he worked for 4 years and then worked with Adlabs for 2 years before he started iRock. Today he is the leading the pack of Story adaptations from spicy novels and enchanting stories and is helping writers and authors get their master piece adapted on screen through his startup #StoryInks, Mumbai, India.

Millions of Indians flock to Bollywood to become a star. The glamour, the glitz, the rush, and of course the money,

Bollywood has it all. Siddhartha Jain, an MBA in finance also had Bollywood dreams, but not to be a movie star.

"Way back in 2000, I had my first startup, a web portal called bollywoodauction. com, which I sold to baazee.com (now taken over by ebayindia.com) and shifted base to work for a Hollywood company in Los Angeles. After an awesome stint, I came back to Mumbai and worked with Mr. Manmohan Shetty in Adlabs Films Ltd."

Dr Manmohan Shetty is a celebrity and highly idolized in Bollywood. He is the founder of Adlab Films Ltd. He has worked with films like Ardh Satya, Gangaajal and Namastey London. He set up the first IMAX and the first Multiplex in India. More recently he has set up the Rs 1,650 Crore Adlabs Imagica on the lines of Universal Studios. Dr Shetty has always backed entrepreneurs and given them a free hand to pursue their innovative dreams without interference, something which does not come very easily to celebrities.

Siddharth further continues "While working with Adlabs, I always had this burning passion within me to start my own film company. After having worked in Hollywood, I was keen that we in India also have a similar experience of film- making and hence, with my company, I wanted to bring about that change in India. I pitched my idea to Mr. Shetty and, fortunately for me, he agreed to fund me and this is how I got my first round of funding and IRock films was on a roll."

Setting up a film production house is a costly affair. But money is not the only issue here. To stand out in Bollywood (Indian Film Industry), you need not only deep pockets, but deep connections. With Manmohan as his backer, he was not only getting the funds but also the credibility and the contacts of a legend like Manmohan Shetty.

With the investment, Dr Shetty also brought in other benefits in kind. "Mr. Shetty allowed me to use his office space for my company and as mentioned, offered me funds which would last as my capital for the next 2 years of operations and so in 2008, iRock Films was born."

The intangibles of this approach of funding are the icing on the cake. Premium office space, contacts, advice, access to otherwise unapproachable icons, all of them reduce

the initial funds required and also increase the chances of success.

In 2009, IRock India worked on RAGINI MMS(One of the most successful films of that year) which was launched under the Balaji Telefilms banner. Taran Adarsh from Bollywood Hungama gave it 4/5 stars and called it a "creepy, spine-chilling date movie" saying, "Ragini MMS amalgamates components of horror, paranormal and sex seamlessly. It titillates, it petrifies, but most importantly, it tells you a story which is daunting, imaginative and unconventional."

"I managed to complete the shoot of Ragini MMS in 12 days with a limited budget and fortunately my bet paid off. After Ragini MMS was a commercial Success, the scene at IRock changed for the better and all the faith invested in me by my investor Mr. Shetty and my team, was ably paid off" concludes Siddharth.

In hindsight, this approach of celebrity funding looks like a no brainer, but I have not seen too many entrepreneurs taking this approach. Raising funds from somebody in the industry, especially with an iconic status does not seem to happen too often.

Stealing of their idea seems to be the number one concern among entrepreneurs. What if the successful guy steals my idea? What prevents him from stealing my idea and using it to build his own company? The vested interest of a person from the same industry is something, which many entrepreneurs are not able to come to terms with. An entrepreneur described going to a successful icon as 'Aa Bail Mujhe Maar' (Digging your own grave) meaning inviting trouble on to you. If the idea is not good, he will not fund it, and if the idea is good, he may probably steal it.

Siddharth ridicules this. Howard H Aiken said 'Don't worry about people stealing an idea. If it's original, you will have to ram it down their throats. "Mr Shetty is himself an entrepreneur and he has worked with a lot of entrepreneurs and helped them. I think he has enough brilliant ideas of his own to waste his time stealing mine".

What else should we know of this "Celebrity" route to funding?

"It's always good to have your homework in place. You just cannot wake up one day and say I want to do this and fund me. I worked hard in this field for good 7-8 years and then I pitched my idea to Mr. Shetty, who, based on my experience and trust on me, funded me."

"Having a good idea with a good business plan is a good idea. It makes sense if you have a good commercially viable plan and your fundamentals in place. Secondly, the team that you form must be a team that relates with it and are not working just for the sake of working. When I started off, I ensured that my team is a set of people who have fire in their belly to achieve things. This spirit of my team helped me a lot. When I wanted to make Ragini MMS, I was restricted by a limited budget of 1 CR and I had to do everything within that limited budget, like shooting, location cost, star payments, production costs etc and so, as a team, I had to slash 50% of my staff salary for one year so that we could manage the budget of Ragini MMS and therefore I feel that a good team coupled with a good business idea is essential."

This is most probably the biggest challenge in getting funded from somebody successful from the industry – a celebrity. Having been there and done that, it is very tough to convince an icon that your idea is original and you will be able to successfully execute it. An idea, which will seem great to a financial investor, will be torn to smithereens by the industry expert. The knowledge of the industry comes with the knowledge of the challenges involved, which makes successful icons very skeptical of new ideas. 'Believe me this won't work. I have already tried it' seems to be the biggest refrain of king makers. Therefore, before you approach the investor, do your homework.

Successful people are also difficult to work with. They can become a pain in the ass with their continuous advice, their know-it-all attitude and their resistance to change. From my perspective, the biggest negative of raising money from successful people is their continuous interference. Startups are all about trying new and innovative approaches and this, more often than not, is in direct conflict with the celebrity's approach. While this can, to some extent, be mitigated by setting expectations right in the beginning of the relationship, some amount of interference is unavoidable. Therefore, startups looking at this approach should be very careful while selecting the investor and do a detailed check on his nature. You are basically looking at him giving you the money and the rolodex. But if there is a whiff that he is interested in getting into daily operations, then it makes sense to avoid this route.

Successful people tend to also get bored very easily. I know a number of cases where a veteran has suddenly parted ways with a startup because he has found something more interesting. Remember, you are just a small fry for him. Your relevance to him is very little, especially in the initial stages, so there is always a chance that the funding might get cut off abruptly. It is therefore, wise in this route of funding to try to pick up money upfront rather than in tranches. Commitment on paper means little; money in the bank is what matters in this case.

While in this route of funding it seems very obvious to maximize the usage of your sponsor's resources, try to avoid it as much as possible. It is always preferable to have a separate office space where you do not have to regularly meet your investor. Also reduce your dependency on the mentor and try as much as possible to create your own network. Bunch up all your advisory requests and meet the investor in a scheduled meeting once or twice a month. The more you keep your distance, the more you will avoid conflict. Remember he is a biggie with more muscle power and a name in the industry. If he gets pissed off, he can screw your happiness big time, so the more you create your own path, the better off you are.

Celebrity Funding:

Pros:
Quick decision by the celebrity
Benefits in kind – office space, resources, advice Contacts in the Industry
Initial Break

Cons:
Interference by the celebrity in daily operations Trying to steer the startup in his direction Risk of losing interest
Backlash in case of conflict

Unlike Financial Investors who have a clear reason to invest in startups, celebrities don't seem to have an obvious reason to invest in startups. Money cannot be the only reason as they have enough of it anyways. So why would a successful icon fund a startup? Kishore Biyani (see the callout) we can understand. He is mostly investing into reasonably established brands and that also as a company for pure financial returns. But why would Mr. Manmohan Shetty fund a startup in exactly the same space and that which could potentially become a threat later.

"Had you known Mr. Shetty, you would have got the answer yourself. The kind of person he is, he is like god for me. An utterly sober and patient person, he encouraged me and the most important thing was, he trusted me. It is his passion for entrepreneurship which made him invest in me," says Siddharth.

Many investors, like Anupam Mittal of Shaadi.com, Deep Karla of Make My Trip.com and Rajan Anandan of Google India (source: Indianangelnetwork.com) to name a few, also seem to have warmed up to this idea and are keen to invest in startups.

The strongest reason for icons to invest in startups seems to be to take the roller coaster ride again but with brakes. The thrill value of once again being part of a small garage startup and, of course, the impossibility of them starting all over again seems to excite many icons to invest in newcomers who might become the next big story. Like Bollywood directors who are proud of their finds, icons also get a great kick from being able to claim they were part of the next Facebook.

Kishore Biyani with his Future Venture seems to have perfected the art of investing in industry startups. He has primarily invested in Ventures which are in spaces related to his business and has got handsome returns. 5.5 times in Biba, 24 times in And Designs and 3.2 times in Capital Foods.

So, now that it is almost Five years since this escapade and the rolling out of his venture, what is his take on the opportunities and risks for this source of celebrity funding?-

"Firstly, the funds came from Mr. Shetty, who is a known name in the film circuit and hence the news that he is my investor tremendously helped me to gain customer confidence in me.

It definitely helped me in leveraging myself better.

Secondly, he being an established and great film maker, he understood the nuances of film making and hence gave me a free hand to work on my projects and never bothered me or interfered in my work. This is what was the best part" says Siddharth.

Any risks that he felt was evident in the funding -

"Not really, I don't think there were any risks. In fact it was a matter of pride to have received support from someone so big. Obviously, it also depends from person to person, but by and large, I was lucky enough to get all the positives from Mr. Shetty. In case of others who were not as lucky as I was, may be the constant interference, the habit of always poking, the pressure to repay the money and lastly, the fear of losing faith in the market, if you fail to repay, is very scary. But I am sure with all determination and confidence, if you opt for this method, you can really do wonders" concludes Siddharth.

Will he try this approach again -

"Yes, of course, I will do it again, but I will now work on some aspects which I had not done in my first stint.

Firstly, I would take funding which would last for at least 3-4 years as 2 years is a very short period. 3-4 years bracket will give me a chance to come over my gestation period and establish myself strongly.

Secondly, I would definitely be more careful of my overheads and consciously ensure that I keep them low and build a team that will stick around with you through thick and thin. Although `I did do that, I would be more careful.

Lastly, I would adopt the blue ocean strategy, where in I would premarket (before launching in market officially) my product, which I did earlier also, but this time I would be more aggressive as that would give me a better mileage.

Siddharth did not let his celebrity investor down. After five years of bumpy ride, he is now growing as a leading cinema production house with various projects lined up in India and abroad and Siddharth is very confident of having his IPO soon and going even bigger. Hats off to IRock Films. Great going!

He has also continued with a similar style of investors. After the success of Ragini MMS, he went ahead and raised his second round of funding from DAR Motion Pictures. DAR operates a fully integrated production and distribution house with offices in India, Dubai and has the hit film, The Lunchbox, to its credit. And then he did it again. He picked up another round from Shravan Shroff of Shringar Films, who sold his multiplex chain Fame Adlabs to INOX Leisure.

No wonder Siddharth and Bollywood seem to go together. Once you get your formula right, keep repeating it again and again.

Fund-O- Drama

Funding Technique - **Celebrity (A renowned person in your industry) Funding**

Prerequisites: Good relationship with your funder (celebrity in question), min. 4- 5 years of experience in the relevant industry, good homework of the field, well laid out business plan, quotient of enthusiasm high.

Time to fund	Less More
Ease of Raising Funds	Easy Difficult
Amount you can Raise	Small Amount Large Amount

2

Mr. Sai Gundavelli

 Born in Hyderabad, Sai came to USA in 1986. He is currently the CEO of one of the leading IT companies in the Valley and he has an inspiring story to tell. Solix Technologies Inc. has been relentlessly working towards delivering groundbreaking enterprise data management solutions. Their flagship product, The Solix Common Data Platform (Solix CDP), has pioneered the concept of unifying all enterprise data (Legacy, Inactive and Active data) of all types (structured and unstructured) in a single, scalable and compliant data platform for infrastructure optimization, ILM, data security and advanced analytics. This is empowering organizations to unleash data-driven applications for improved customer engagement, operational efficiency and profitability.

"I decided to come to the US in 1986 to pursue my Master's in Mechanical from University of Oklahoma" says Sai, the founder of the multi-million-dollar company, "The reason I applied there was because of the application fee cost and I am happy I enrolled as I bagged a scholarship for my master's program." Given the oil crisis, things were indeed very tough, but Sai had his vision in place. He was sure he would be the different one. "No one in my family had ever tried their hand in business but I was sure I would have my own business someday" says Sai proudly.

After completing his Masters, Sai joined a company called Arix Corporation. He worked there for some time and moved to Cisco. Fate had its own outcome, and he became a millionaire, literally.

"I was one of the lucky few who had the rare opportunity to cash in on my stock options. Cisco stocks were sky rocketing and I found this as an opportunity to fulfill my dreams" says Sai with a sparkle.

Sai used the funding from his stock options and started his own company in 1996. Since at Cisco he had worked on Oracle ERP implementation, he too decided to enter the same domain and began a journey never to look back upon. "I funded and began my company in 1996 with the money from stock options and have never had to look back" beams Sai with confidence. Stock options then and now can turn around fortunes, especially when the stock prices are sky rocketing, paying patrons royally for their loyalty. For instance, Facebook has made many employees millionaires from stock options. The spectacular success of Silicon Valley companies and the resulting economic riches of employees who held stock options have made Stock Option Plans a powerful motivational tool for employees to work for the company's long-term success.

An article in the all Business journal by Mr. Richard Harrock talks about Stock Option and how it works.

The following shows how stock options are granted and exercised:

- ABC, Inc., hires employee John Smith.

- As part of his employment package, ABC grants John options to acquire 40,000 shares of ABC's common stock at 25 cents per share (the fair market value of a share of ABC common stock at the time of grant).

- The options are subject to a four-year vesting with one-year cliff vesting, which means that John has to stay employed with ABC for one year before he gets the right to exercise 10,000 of the options and then he vests the remaining 30,000 options at the rate of 1/36 a month over the next 36 months of employment.

- If John leaves ABC or is fired before the end of his first year, he doesn't get any of the options.

- After his options are "vested" (become exercisable), he has the option to buy the stock at 25 cents per share, even if the share value has gone up dramatically.

- After four years, all 40,000 of his option shares are vested if he has continued to work for ABC.

- ABC becomes successful and goes public. Its stock trades at $20 per share.

- John exercises his options and buys 40,000 shares for $10,000 (40,000 x 25 cents).

- John turns around and sells all 40,000 shares for $800,000 (40,000 x the $20 per share publicly traded price), making a nice profit of $790,000.

Th math here is so exciting. Starting your own dream venture with funds from your stock option- that's simply amazing! Back then, when the IT boom was somewhat catching up, a decision like this is phenomenal because it reflects your passion. Most of us would probably have decided to park the money in safe compartments and save them for our rainy days. But Sai didn't do that, he not only invested that money into his dream venture but was also futuristic enough to tie in the resources of India and opened an office in Hyderabad. He started to deploy the Oracle ERP for his clients and grew the company to a 200 plus strong workforce just in a matter of few years.

"Those were some days. I was new to business, but I had the right team who helped in managing, and everything was going great for me" remembers Sai. But the ship rocked at some point and it did pose some challenges for Sai.

"In the year 2001-02, the dotcom bubble crashed and so did the markets. The shares of Cisco that I was left with dropped down significantly and it did put a huge indent on my workings. But the good part was I managed to have some parallel investments made which saved some of my finances" says Sai. Customers started looking for offshore vendors for ERP Services and we had to reinvent ourselves as we were primarily a US company.

Despite this tremor, Sai pulled through. Google back then was not the company it is today, and Sai found in them a suitable partner for the Enterprise search technology. As he was working with Google, he realized that there was indeed a lot of Enterprise data that had to be dealt with and this helped him make his most important decision of creating some platform that can help them manage Enterprise data. This seed of a thought quickly helped Sai transform his current company to a new avatar called Solix Technologies and in 2002, Sai was heading the company which was to achieve amazing milestones going forward.

"I realized people wanted to capture a lot of data for Artificial Intelligence and Machine Learning and that triggered me to dive into the space of Enterprise data management." Sai further adds "I based my business model on helping companies to be data-driven."

But with the rocky market conditions, how did Sai manage to generate funds and what did he do to ensure that his seed of thought germinates into something concrete? To this he says "I was falling short of funds owing to the world crisis we were in and hence I took some external investment from corporate investors and high net worth individual friends and invested in Solix to enable the company to work robustly in this space."

Sai took his first major external funding and ensured he stretched every penny that he has to invest.

"I was once again on track and I ensured I designed my products and services in a manner most appropriate to growth."

And he did grow; with a strength of 250 plus employees, global customer base, a leader in Gartner Magic Quadrant and selling his products to some of the top-rated companies all over the world, Solix for sure had arrived.

Today Solix proudly partners with some of the best names in the Valley like Amazon, Cloudera, Microsoft, IBM and Oracle, to name a few. When you have external investors, dynamics are different, and this is also echoed by Sai. When you have investors from the Valley, they bring more value, it becomes smart money.

Solix therefore has been fortunate to have had two different kinds of funding. One, at a personal level through Sai's Cisco employee stock options and the other through corporate investors and friends. Both were at different levels and timeframes. "It is always different to have some funding from folks in Silicon Valley, vis a vis funds from non-valley folks" laughs Sai and continues "smart money". It was just not another investment, that investment came with a good Board.

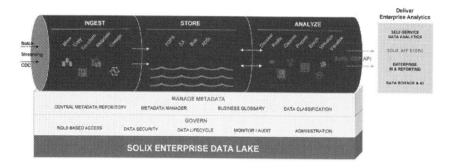

So, will Sai ever repeat this type of funding?

"Yes, always, because I feel investors bring good ideas and advice on board and your chances of success obviously improves" says Sai.

That would certainly mean that he recommends this type of funding to others?

"Yes, of course. If your family and friends invest in you that means you are on the right track and it kind of prepares you for the funding you may seek from others outside your orbit," says Sai and continues "As far as Cisco funding is concerned, I was very fortunate to have that kind of significant mileage on my stocks. I also believed in myself and was sure I will be successful. So, anyone in my place, if they have got this fortune and have ever dreamt of being an entrepreneur should chart out this roadmap for themselves."

So, does that mean the entrepreneur should be a little vigilant or careful before starting a venture and using the funds?

"Entrepreneurship is sexy, and everybody is attracted to it, but not everyone can do this. I strongly believe in the 80/20 principle. 80% is what you want and why you want. Put 80% of your time on what you want to do and why you want to do and why you will be successful with self-introspection and thorough venture research. Once you are convinced and want to go ahead, spend the amount equivalent to the balance 20% and invest and move ahead and work on the modalities of success and how you can make that happen." Says Sai.

This makes complete sense; an entrepreneur needs to build a solid foundation before aiming for funding else he/she may get out of the race in the very first lap and that could cause distress and discouragement.

Sai has been in the valley for 20 plus years now and he has seen the valley roar and has had the experiences few would be lucky to have, especially when the Silicon Valley contributes a significant chunk to the real GDP of the country and has a massive scope for global competence.

Sai further states "I don't mean to discourage but entrepreneurship is not for everyone. If you choose to be an entrepreneur, have the patience, courage and tenacity. Do not lose patience. Always base your decisions on data and analysis and ensure that decisions are made accordingly."

Sai has for sure learned, experienced and worked his way through and brought Solix to a level where its existence speaks for itself. Success has no short-cuts. Always stand by your convictions, work hard, give it your all, and the rest will follow.

Fund-O- Drama

Funding Technique – **Funding through Associate/Friend**

Prerequisites: Own capital, robust business plan, clear vision, ability to manage risk.

Time to fund	
	Less More
Ease of fund	
	Low High
Amount	
	Less More

3

Lambent Technologies

 Lambent Technologies was founded as an IT services company in 2000. It was a pioneer in IT services in Nagpur, India. It grew to a large end to end Software Solutions Company with operations in San Diego, Chicago, Mumbai and Nagpur. In 2006, it was acquired by 'Globallogic' an 'Outsorced Product Engineering Services Company, which itself was subsequently acquired by Apax Partners, one of the largest PE funds.

Former Founder: Shashikant Choudhary

 Visionary, Entrepreneur, Professor, Guru, God.Ask an IT professional in Nagpur and they consider Shashi the pioneer of the IT revolution in Nagpur. He is one of the very few professionals who, even after making their fortune, still stuck to their hometown and continued contributing to the growth of Nagpur. He works with a lot of Technology startups, helping them with space, guidance and money to become the next Infosys or TCS.

'Employee Stock Option Plan' is something which every IT professional is familiar with. It is a great tool for rewarding employees, but what if you want the reverse – not to give but take money from your employees. In 2000, one man in Nagpur twisted this concept upside down and created an Employee Stock Selling Option.

Using this unique and original scheme, he created a pool of investors out of his own employees and funded his company 'Lambent Technologies' to become a large player in the Information Technology space.

Employee Stock Options Scheme or ESOP is a scheme under which Employees get stocks of their company at highly discounted prices. The most successful example of ESOP is Infosys Technologies who gave away over $10Bn worth of shares and made millionaires of hundreds of its employees. ESOP is considered a proven strategy for startups to retain employees and reduce cost of training, recruitment and lost opportunities. Hundreds of IT companies, especially startups, have used this very effectively to retain and grow talent.

Meet Shashi Chaudhary, a pioneer in IT Education in Nagpur having formed the first Computer Tech Department at YCCE Nagpur. In 2000, the entrepreneur bug finally caught up with him and he started his venture right out of Nagpur.

"I started Lambent technologies, providing IT services and support to my clients, with my seed capital of 2 lakhs. These 2 lakhs were out of my personal savings and some more money came from a couple of my relatives. I started off with a bang in the year 2000 with 6 employees that I recruited at that time." remembers Shashi, smiling at the thought of his early days.

He goes on "After I kick started my venture, I realized I needed to pump in more money and so I explored the various traditional routes of funding - Bank Loans, Mortgages, VC (Venture Capitalist) Funding and Angel Funding but somehow they did not appeal to me. The fact that we would do all the work and somebody else would benefit was not something very palatable. And I did not want to saddle my company with high interest rates of banks. I had read a lot of these ESOP schemes and suddenly it struck me, My most valuable resources were my employees, why not partner with them itself? Why don't I pitch for investments to my employees? I did not need a very big amount and so I could easily ask each one of them to pump in one lakh to five lakh each. But the question was why would they do so? What value proposition would I give them which would benefit them?"

He continues "By this time, this idea had taken me over and I started designing a strategy to woo employees and then suddenly the idea of 'Employee Stock Selling Option' dawned on me where I would offer stocks of my company to the employees at a certain face value. But that would not be enough. Me being a startup, why would they value my stock and pay upfront for it. To ensure I instill a 'Wow' factor in this approach, I decided to add an extra hook for my employees. The highlight was that the employee would have the option of selling 10% stock from his holdings back to company every 3 months and hence this option was aptly named 'Employee Stock Selling Option'. That meant that the employee could redeem all his shares in a span of about two and a half years."

While the approach of Shashi is radical, it is not unprecendented. A somewhat similar model has been used by Gujarat Co-operative Milk Marketing Federation Ltd., more commonly known as Amul. Amul was formed in 1946 as a cooperative and is today owned by more than three million milk producers of Gujarat in India. This model helped it keep the company intact and become the largest food brand in India.

Unlike ESOP, which is only a retention tool, Shashi had created a plan, which was both an ESOP plus a source of funds. But it seems like a nerve racking way of funding a company. Imagine a sword hanging over your head, which will drop every three months. Not only would he have to pay off his stakeholders every three months, he would have to keep creating a better and better valuation of the company to ensure that the employees would redeem their stocks. Otherwise he would be stuck with employees who would neither be interested in working with him nor sell out their stocks. I am quite sure that Shashi had not figured out all the implications of his Employee Stock Selling Option or he might have thought twice before trying such an audacious approach.

Shashi smiles remembering those times, "I pumped in money every 3 months from my relatives and friends who were based out of various places in the world and doing very well in their professions. Since I enjoyed a brilliant personal creditability with them, I kept borrowing funds from each one of them and as for them; it was a meager amount so they didn't mind it. Using this money I was able to regularly pay off the employees and at the same time keep growing the company. My stakeholders became my biggest strength. Since they had a vested interest in the valuation of the company, they went all out to grow the company. Together we were able to take Lambent to a valuation of 200,000 USD in a span of just two years.

I was successfully able to return back the money to the employees with handsome returns every three months."

Interesting! Since Shashi came up with this brilliant way of leveraging his startup, what does he feel were the major pros of this source of funding?-

"This process helped me to firstly retain my employees.

Secondly, it helped the employees generate some liquidity over and above their salary which again was fruitful for them, which was happening every 3 months.

Thirdly, the employee realized the potential and value of the company which proved very beneficial for the company."

The biggest advantage of funding through employees, as Shashi has pointed out, is the ability to retain employees. The year 2000 was when dot coms were booming and it was really tough to find good IT people. Moreover, since the employees are also stakeholders, they are usually willing to work at a discount to the market (compared to the market rate) and are not comparing their salaries with their peers on a day to day basis.

Also in a way, Shashi had created a whole pool of people who had a vested interest in the success of the company. This meant a dedicated, committed and self-motivated task force. Shashi was no more the sole entrepreneur, he had created a whole set of mini entrepreneurs.

This approach is also suitable for only small amounts of money and where you need a dedicated talented team – perfect for IT Products or services. Assuming an average of five lakhs per employee and ten employees, this approach seems best for raising up to fifty lakhs. However, there are also benefits in kind. Lesser salaries and dramatic reduction in hiring and firing costs can make a startup much more competitive and nimble, compared to its competitors. The confidence that your employees will be with you for a long time can help you take bolder and longer decisions. This is what helped Shashi spread his wings beyond India in the western countries.

The flip side of this approach is also pretty obvious.

"The biggest risk of this approach is the reputation loss I would suffer in case I could not keep my commitments. The 'Damocles' sword was perpetually hanging over my head. In a normal startup, if you can't make it successful, you may suffer personal losses but your reputation is not at stake. Here, I had made promises to fresh people just out from college and I was too scared to imagine what would happen if I could not meet my commitments. One commitment not met, and I could lose all my employees. And with this reputation no new employee would join me. So I had to keep going on and ensuring that every three months I had the money to pay them off. Oh, this is something challenging but not difficult if one is persistent enough."

There are many additional challenges beyond reputation to this approach.

Interference from the minor stakeholders could become quite painful. Once an employee starts thinking he is a part owner of the company, he could become quite demanding and wants to be part of all the decisions of the company, I have seen various startups where minority stakeholders have started questioning the value of the main promoter and started demanding larger shareholdings in proportion to the main shareholder & so one has to tread this path carefully. To mitigate this risk, Shashi suggests offering this option to only a few employees and only at the start of the venture. Too many stakeholders could become inconvenient later on. Also, he suggests that this approach works best with a young talent pool, especially freshers out of good colleges. Younger people are more open minded and work much better with such approaches.

Then there are technical challenges. What if the employee leaves after three months? Will he retain all his shares or will he have to return them back. What if the promoter is not able to buy back the shares in three months – is the employee then entitled to sell the shares to somebody else? What are the taxation implications on such a scheme since, while the Indian Income tax act sets out guidelines for an ESOP scheme, there are no equivalent guidelines for a Employee Stock Selling Scheme? In the end it, worked out fine for Shashi. But one default from Shashi and it could become a legal minefield.

> Funding from your employees:
>
> Pros:
> Funds can be raised quickly.
> Dedicated and committed team with a sense of ownership. Benefits in kind – Lower salaries, low attrition cost.
> Long term bets can be taken.
>
> Cons:
> Constant pressure to grow. Can become very challenging. You can only raise a small amount.
> High risk of reputation loss.
> Backlash in case you do not meet your commitments.

So will Shashi try this approach again? -

"Yes, of course I will, since it has proved to be very beneficial to me and I got the opportunity to merge with a mammoth company like 'GlobalLogic Inc' based out of USA only on my exemplary ways of sourcing funds and thereby creating a valuable company for all. However, the next time, I will also include the option of 'Employee Stock Buying Option' where the employees will have the choice of increasing their worth by buying more stocks and also as a typical case, the newer ones who join, can simply buy and sell stocks as per their wish".

In 2006, Lambent Technologies was acquired by 'GlobalLogic', a company based out of USA, but started by four Indians. 'Lambent Technologies' eventually became

'Globallogic's Center of Excellence for Mobile Products'. Shashi himself joined GlobalLogic as the 'Managing Director of GolbalLogic India operations'.

Shashi feels that his approach to business and his unique way of funding were key drivers in this acquisition and his subsequent appointment as Managing Director. In October 2013, 'Apax Partners', one of the largest PE funds completely took over GlobalLogic and Shashi got handsomely rewarded for the amazing venture he had started in 2000 with a handful of employee stakeholders.

To conclude, I would like to replicate a beautiful statement made by Peter Harrison, President & CEO of Snagajob on linkedin.

Shashi is a great teacher, entrepreneur and leader. His passion for people and technology is unbridled. He's a forward thinking and fearless visionary who attracts and weaves together close, knit teams that work well together, grow together and rarely ever leave. Like all great leaders, he's socially minded and big hearted. Not only is he a founding father of the technology sector in Nagpur, but he has also put both, the city and Global Logic permanently on the map of the global mobile ecosystem and both are indebted t to him.

Fund-O- Drama

Funding Technique – **Funding through your employees**

Prerequisites: Talented and young employee base, High Personal creditability in friends and family, Creating company capability to buy employee stock periodically.

Time to fund	Less More
Ease of Raising Funds	Easy Difficult
Amount you can Raise	Small Amount Large Amount

4

Get through Guides

Get through Guides (GTG) is a publishing, training and content development company, which produces high quality books/materials at affordable prices in the fields of finance, accounting and management. Get through Guides also trains professionals across the globe to pass professional certifications using revolutionary and transformational methods. With centers in the UK and in India, their trainers move around the globe.

GTG writes materials for the Insurance Institute of India, the Indian insurance regulator, IRDA and many other professional institutes around the globe. Over 1 million people in India alone are using GTG's textbooks.

Founder: Vandana Saxena Poria OBE

Vandana Saxena Poria qualified as a UK Chartered Accountant with HW Fisher. After qualifying, she spent 10 years living and working in a multitude of countries in Central and Eastern Europe. She initially worked for Ernst & Young. She went on to become the CEO of BPP International, the international division of Europe's largest listed professional training company with a turnover in excess of £160 million. In this capacity, she was responsible for all training outside the UK. She was also responsible for drafting the first versions of the IFRS and ISA material for BPP. Vandana was also an Award-winning trainer and passionate speaker, be it on women, inspiration or IFRS.

Vandana also works closely with the British Government to foster international trade for the UK and has given numerous presentations for/to the UKTI. She has held several positions with the British Chambers of Commerce in several countries including that of Chairperson. She is a Director and board member of the UK India

Business Council. In 2008, Vandana was honored with an OBE (equivalent of the Padmashri) from Her Majesty the Queen, one of the youngest Asian females to be honored).

For most organizations, a servicing arm of a company could mean an after sales division of an engineering company, or it could be an arm of business supporting the core one. In Vandana's case, it was the latter. For her, this title could aptly be used for a services industry firm, which uses some temporary means of services to fund one's core activity. In Vandana's case, the servicing arm at that given point of time were the services of training that she started providing as a strategy to leverage some funds, which they could use for their core business activity: the production of high profile books for various professional Accountancy and BFSI exams and other important subjects at an affordable price.

"As a strategic division of our company, we started training people to generate cash and help in our marketing. We decided that we will let our students speak for us and market us obviously if they have liked us and so we started driving our training function with all the enthusiasm," says Vandana.

She further continues, "Writing books is a cash intensive exercise. You have to pay the authors, proof readers and designers upfront and you only get the cash if the books sell. For the first year, our company was in an incubation mode as we were all busy developing content for the books for people to learn from. We kept feeding our earnings from the services arm into the expenses of writing these books and worked for a year to develop content. Our main goal was to launch text books on various topics for the international exams and hence content development was the heart. If people could pass the exams because the books were easy to understand, we would have met our goal." says Vandana

Vandana scaled her business through her training division and kept the show going on. By that time, her content development work was also in line and the time came when she needed real big money to launch her textbooks to the market for people to learn and compete in the international standard exams.

"Yes, although training today for GTG is a full time activity, at that time, it was used as a servicing arm to begin my company and to fund it more necessarily" says Vandana.

Since Vandana started funding her core activity of producing high quality books for training purposes, was delivering training an irrelevant activity at that time?

"Not irrelevant, but yes, it was something GTG never aspired to increase its bandwidth on. We always wanted to have our publishing, developing on high quality books to be our core activity, which we achieved also. But the achievement came in place because we had this servicing arm/temporary services funding us. It also served another purpose: we could see how the students reacted to our materials in the classroom. They helped refine our books," quips Vandana.

This is interesting. A servicing arm like this in case of Vandana was not a deterrent to her core since it in a way helped Vandana build her foundation and get her to the level of being marketable in the mega funding scenario. But there could be a small hiccup of distributing one's resources ably amongst the core and the non-core servicing arms since both hold crucial positions on the road map. It could be as simple as dividing the time and hence the question of time management would have been difficult for Vandana to manage.

"Time was divided as per the situation. I did it phase wise. I knew that my servicing arm could bring in the funds for my core so I had my core activity decided as per the funds I made. If I had the available funds ready with me for investing appropriately to take it to the next level, I would slow down my servicing arm a bit and concentrate on the core activity again till the time it was stable and ready to move onto the next stage," assures Vandana.

This is good. The servicing arm, being this exemplary source of funding and complementing the core can be accelerated and slowed as per one's choice as we have seen in case of Vandana. I am sure her employees too did not have much to worry, or hopefully while doing this, they did not nick off their heads being all confused as to which one they should concentrate more on-the core or the servicing arm.

'No, that was not the case. Firstly, I had very employees on my roll. Secondly, the training delivery aspects of my servicing arm were ably taken care of by the trainers I had aligned with and hence as per requirement they would go and deliver.

Thirdly, the employees of my core activity would come into action only when the phase of action would demand of them. In the meantime, they would slowly and soundly build on our foundation which proudly stands today in the name of GTG," explains Vandana.

The phase wise model as explained by Vandana of balancing her core and her servicing arm would have had some impact on her and other promoters. It may have resulted in losing focus or losing some interest since it was not a normal situation.

"It was not like that ever. We knew very clearly where our vision was when we started off and fortunately it was pretty clear, Moreover we were the originators of the idea to fund our core through our servicing arm, so the question of us digressing was not possible," reasons Vandana.

Several instances are there where the servicing arm at one point becomes so lucrative that it becomes the core business of that company. Did Vandana today make training delivery one of her core activities owing to the same reasons?

Vandana says-"Never, as I said earlier, we were very clear since the beginning that we did keep training delivery a temporary service or a servicing arm but later as our core would establish strongly and would self-sustain, we would equally grow our servicing arm, which we did".

The non-core or the servicing arm activity of Vandana never gave an instance to her where she would get lost in it and lose her focus. She knew that the day her core activity would reach the desired level, she would blow the whistle. She did get to that stage when her core activity had slowly reached a stage where she could take it to the next level.

In her case, she had managed the scenario well but, for better management, does she feel that there could be 2 teams formed, one for core and one for the servicing arm?

"I really don't think there are two teams required. Yes, the responsibilities of the core and non-core arms could be divided amongst the existing team and the same should be made very clear to them. This will help them to perform dually and give adequate time to both non-core and core as and when required," explains Vandana.

This probably would lead me to quote a striking example of one of the leading wind energy companies which had the same team for their core and non-core activities. This created a lot of confusion, instability, and firefighting within the team. The agenda of their preference was probably not on the same lines as others and hence, it resulted in the firefighting. Fortunately for GTG, there were no such situations. One has to be very clear of his/her path and agenda to tread ahead and this was something that was ably done and hence the same team could perform and meet desired results.

The idea of funding her core through her servicing arm took Vandana places. She won the angel funding not from India but from the UK, she candidly says in her affirmable style.

"After a year of no investment and funding through my servicing arm, I learnt about a seminar in UK which was to be organized by UK India Business Council and Angel

Investors where I came to know that the participants had an opportunity to pitch themselves to the investors but had a cap of 8 mins to make the impact, which was like finding a sea shell in the sea".

Vandana performed this immaculate task of perfecting the moment that was to be spent in front of the investors meticulously. So was her effort lauded?

She says, "Yes, and bingo, I completed my presentation in 7 minutes and 55 seconds flat, which made quite a impression on them and bang, I got my first round of funding from the UK India Angel funding. I thought that to be an impeccable achievement".

After the splendid process of getting her core funded through non-core, she could finally grab the opportunity of funding through the UK Angel investors and she was head over heels for the same. The internal funding enabled her to build her foundation and pitch herself with full throttle to the UK investors.

"The timelines did ensure that the pressure on you is double. The challenge therefore becomes dual. One, ensuring you complete the presentation with the important turning points and highlights in flat 8 minutes and second, the gigantic task of impressing but I did not budge and decided to tread the path" says Vandana.

Since Vandana could finally manage the funding what was her take on its merits and de merits?

Now that we have seen the pros and cons of the servicing arm funding, let us also have a quick look at some of the merits and demerits of UK angels since we are already discussing that. Also, let's not forget that Vandana could achieve this feat of UK funding only because she could fund her first year through her servicing arm.

So let's have a quick peep into the UK investors. Vandana elaborates-

A, they were very quick in their process and did not take a lot of time in sanctioning.

B, they are very organized. They have such good knowledge of the system that they know what to do when and it proved very beneficial.

C, they are also surprisingly and incredibly supportive, which makes a lot of your work easier. They also guide you and ensure that you on the right track.

Lastly and most importantly they make you do the fair valuation of your company and ask you to not deviate from the same, which again is a good and very rare quality. Based on this valuation they offer you the equity.

Pros-

1) You have a source of funding, which is internal and therefore no burden of interest
2) An ongoing activity, which showcases and establishes your name in the market, even though it may not be your prime activity.
3) You get to use the funds as and when you feel comfortable and there is no defiance of misusage.

Cons-

1) Limited funds as your new arm may not be able to suffice you with all.
2) Limited manpower to concentrate on non-core and core
3) One could get deviated from his core objective unless proper focus and time management is maintained

Owing to all the above merits, it really becomes a nice pitch to bet on and seek funding but like al coins have 2 sides, this kind of funding has its own de-merits, which is that the UK based investors are not very aware of the Indian market conditions and hence, that could prove detrimental for one as the trust which they place in you is questioned, says Vandana.

Vandana, having achieved the funding and experienced the same, is very keen to recommend this to others and says that Indian companies should explore, both from your service arm and the UK investors as that is a real good platform. She says "Although many IT companies are commonly using the technique of raising funds through servicing arm, I would urge other industries also to follow suit."

For UK investors, she just has a word of caution-

"'Please ensure that your paperwork is up to date as they are very particular about it".

"Secondly, please read and understand each clause of the MoU that you sign with the UK angel investors as it will be beneficial to you and will give you more clarity".

Great! Vandana has brought about a whole new knowledge and paradigm shift in funding by introducing the UK angel investors to us.

GTG has an impressive list of clients, which include ICAI, KPMG, Tata, Mahindra, HDFC, Deloitte, Genpact, WNS, IHG as well as a host of colleges and bookshops across five major continents (North America, South America, Africa, Europe and Asia)

They also work closely with various, prestigious professional accountancy institutes around the globe and have been commissioned to develop publications/training for some of them. Recently GTG wrote the entire series of books that the 'Institute of Chartered Accountants of Tanzania' will use to train they CAs. Their aim is to provide the best and, trey have been recognized for their effort by various professional accolades including being certified by Institute around the globe. This recognition strengthens their resolve to continuously strive to provide the best finance and accountancy education.

Fund-O- Drama

Funding Technique – **Funding through your Servicing arm (Non-core)**

Prerequisites: Proper servicing arm option, good team management and time management, and ability to focus equally on the core and the servicing arm business.

Time to fund	
	Less More
Ease of fund	
	Low High
Amount	
	Less More

Fund-O- Drama

Funding Technique – **(UK Angel Investors)**

Pre-requisites: Perfect paper, Strong presentation skills, ability to make the impact in very short? in front of multiple investors.

Time to fund	
	Less More
Ease of fund	
	Low High
Amount	
	Less More

5

iWeb Technology Solutions

iWeb Technology Solutions Pvt. Ltd. is a Private Limited Company incorporated in the year 2005. Using innovative tools, it develops and implements a suite of innovative enterprise applications that operate in an integrated environment and conform to international standards. Although founded as a pure software product/ solutions company, it is strategically diversifying as a software services provider to draw on a growing market that wants "Software as a Service" (SaaS) & "Platform as a Service" (PaaS).

Founder: Akshay Shah

Akshay is a technology & business enthusiast cum blogger. He is an invitee blogger on global platforms like GrowVC.com, Yourstory.in and TechnoFIRST portal respectively. He has been voted & nominated to speak at The People's Stage @ Websummit, Dublin 2013 and iWeb has also been selected for The ALPHA @ www.websummit.net. He has won in the **Software Innovation category of MIT Technology Review's INDIA TR35 2011** contest, which recognizes the outstanding innovators under the age of 35 each year. Akshay has also been conferred with the prestigious honor of "STAR ENTREPRENEURSHIP AWARD" by the "3rd International India Innovation Summit."

2018 - He has recently taken up a honorary position as NASSCOM SMB India West Champion and is also selected as a Mentor under the GOI initiative of 'Atal Innovation Mission – AIM'. He has even recently launched a 'FREEMIUM' model, the 1st of its kind in the industry where he digitizes the operations of an entire University / College / School FOR FREE along with sponsor partners who are large fintechs / banks / Cloud providers such that it's a win win for all.

"Entrepreneurship is like falling in love and dying for it! When you are in love that's all you can see, feel and do, right? If as an Entrepreneur, you do not get sleepless nights for your Love, i.e. the enterprise, idea or business that you have conceived, you are bound to fail!!!

These are the words of Akshay Shah, founder of iWeb technology solutions, Mumbai. For him, it was his love for entrepreneurship which enabled him to start his own web technology company. Akshay began in 2005 after leaving midway his Chartered accountancy course that he was undergoing because as mentioned, he fell in love with entrepreneurship.

"I started out iWeb technology solutions in 2005 with funds from my father and my own savings. My father was a bigger contributor and hence the force behind me and my success today. Although I am a simple B.Com (Bachelors of Commerce) and half CA, I was very keen to start my own venture and I fell in love with this concept. I collaborated with my dad's friend and his professional colleague Mr Ketan Trivedi and together we started this venture iWeb Technology Solutions in 2005" says Akshay.

He further continues "Once I started out with my venture, I managed to bootstrap my show and after 5 years, I started looking for funds and hence approached banks but owing to lack of collateral security, I could not get the bank loan. During those 5 years, I was constantly bootstrapping myself. Whatever little we could manage, we invested in our company and kept the movement going. Since we had limited options, we took 5 years to get funded while bootstrapping, I would also try and present myself to various funders. When I was amidst my thoughts of what should be my next move, I got in touch with this angel investment consultant who was instrumental in getting me the friendly angel funding. But one thing I must add here, in the initial years when I was struggling to get funds, I went pillar to post to VC's, Angel investors, banks and several other places to avail funds but did not get any luck. After my running around, I realized that the attitude of these funders is very different in India as compared to the Silicon Valley where the team that is working on the project and the idea of the project are the two basic criteria that are looked into by the investors outside".

Here's an interesting point made by Akshay, about certain attitudinal differences in Indian mindsets as compared to the ones of Silicon. In the words of Mr. Mohanjit Jolly, Managing Director, Draper Fisher Jurvetson, he has a very interesting take on the same. In 2008, he made a shift from the Silicon Valley to India and based on his experience he had the following pointers-

1. **Getting it going:** The bright-eyed bushy tailed first time entrepreneurs are in abundance both in India and in the US. Quite honestly, those are the risk-taking men and women by whom I am most intrigued. What's interesting is that the definition and embodiment of entrepreneurship is very different between India and the US. I am talking not at the strategic but e tactical level.

2. **Incremental not monumental:** Often entrepreneurs tend to think of a better mousetrap; something that is only incrementally better than the incumbent solution. Silicon Valley entrepreneurs have the luxury of being surrounded by many entrepreneurs who have been part of truly game changing companies. Often those same successful entrepreneurs tend to advise other first-time entrepreneurs to think monumental, not incremental.

In India that is not the case at this time. There aren't many examples of great companies that have been created from scratch (at least on the pure technology front) and an ecosystem of successful entrepreneurs either investing in or advising others to think "disruptive" or "curve jumping", just to use another couple of often used Silicon Valley descriptions. As a result, generally speaking (and this is admittedly a gross generalization), I tend to see a lot more "incremental" than "monumental" and "evolutionary" than "revolutionary" ideas in India than in the US.

A corollary to the above argument is one of thinking at local versus global level. In the US, entrepreneurs often think about a global impact or reach from the get-go. They may not roll out a product or service globally from the very beginning, but the aspirations and the long-term plans, more often than not, include global expansion. In India, thinking global is much more the exception than the rule. That may be due to the non-IP nature of most Indian ventures where competing on the global stage may be difficult because of the fact that the Indian market itself may be large enough or there is a leaser focus on making the company successful at a national level before even thinking about international expansion.

3. **High tech, mid tech, low tech, no tech:** I had a thesis when I moved to India that true technology innovation would start occurring in meaningful way and

new startups with real intellectual property would start taking shape here. I hypothecated that happening via three mechanisms: 1) reverse brain drain or folks moving back to India from the US primarily after getting the successful startup bug there; 2) teams departing IT services companies or multinational R&D centers in India after seeing a lot more potential (financially and otherwise) by being entrepreneurs rather than part of a large company; and 3) ideas being incubated within academia and being spun out. All three are happening, but still in infancy. Indian startups often involve an idea that has been successful elsewhere in the world and "Indianizing" it. In the US, I always used the three T's for decision making: Team, Technology (IP) and Traction within a large market. In India, the decision making is based more on the team and their execution capability.

4. **Retention and Churn:** I thought hiring and retaining talent was a tough task in Silicon Valley-until I came to India. The challenge is far greater for Indian entrepreneurs than for their Silicon Valley counterparts.

In India, employees are much more cash conscious and as such, place little to no value on options in their respective companies. Regulatory hurdles like the FBT have not helped either. Two key sets of events have to happen to engrain loyalty and curtail churn-significant layoffs at bell weather Indian firms and wealth creation through exits in venture funded startups. And both will happen in due time.

5. **Dearth of seed:** Although the venture capital ecosystem is very well established in the Silicon Valley, the same is just starting to take shape in India. When I say ecosystem, I mean a cohesive network of investors, service providers, banks (fewer of them as of now), academia and larger corporations, all looking to engage with entrepreneurs in a meaningful way.

Within the investor group, there are various tiers from angel groups, seed and truly early stage funds, to mid stage and late stage/growth stage private equity firms who have both formal and informal relationships in place to transition a startup from "womb to tombstone". Let me focus on the seed capital segment of the investor food chain for a minute.

Getting the initial capital is often the biggest catch-22 for a startup. One needs capital to show traction, but investors often look for that traction before they commit capital. That is precisely where the angel groups and seed/early stage funds come into play. They often invest when there isn't much, if any, traction and the investment is in an idea and the team that has the confidence and background to execute a big vision.

Seed capital is again more readily available in Silicon Valley than it is in India. There are angel groups like the Band of Angels, Silicon Valley Angels, Angels Forum etc, along with super angels like Andy Bechtelsheim, the Google guys, and many other seasoned executives who readily write $100,000 checks to get companies going.

Service providers and others are willing to help entrepreneurs early on, not for cash but for equity in their companies or a combination of cash and equity. In India, that seeding infrastructure is nowhere close to being robust, but Kudos to entities like the Seed Fund, Erasmic/Accel, Mumbai Angels etc. who are trying to fill that void.

But most existing and new entrants are targeting primarily later stage investments due to the risk reduction and shorter liquidity horizon. For the venture capital community and environment to thrive, that movement towards later stage investments will have to change. It's clear that unless there is high quality seed stage ventures being funded, the deal funnel will be fairly dry for those chasing later stage opportunities.

Venture funds in India will most likely have to adopt a bi-modal investment distribution with a combination of early stage and mid-late stage investments. DFJ has done its part with seed stage investments relatively recently in several companies including MGinger, Canvera, Catura and Attero.

Akshay adds to this. "You know here in India, we still talk the balance sheet language and don't go beyond that. Gone are the days when idea could get you the necessary funds as now what is more important is your history, your balance sheet and all of this is well assessed by these VC's and hence on a lighter note I call these VC's as Vulture Capitalists and not Venture capitalists," says Akshay laughingly.

Vulture Capitalists!! That sounds interesting.

The words 'Vulture Capitalists' are sparingly used as slang for a venture capitalist that deprives an inventor of control over his or her own innovations and most of the money the inventor should have made from the invention. This may be why Akshay calls them vulture capitalist. In contrast, the friendly angel investors, as in the case of Akshay, seem to be more lucrative an option. But why? What is it that differentiates them from the ferocious vulture capitalists?

In the words of Rosemary Peavler, a retired college professor of Business Finance from Morehead State University where she taught for 25 years, the process of friendly angel investors and Venture Capitalists has a sea of differences as below-

- She says that contrary to popular belief, venture capitalists seldom provide start-up funding to entrepreneurial ventures. Angel investors, on the other hand, exist to provide seed financing to start-up ventures. Angel investors are willing to take on the risk of a brand new firm, where venture capitalists prefer to become involved a little later down the line.

- Angel investing is perhaps the more mysterious of the two forms of equity financing. Angel investing is a very old term harkening back to the 1920's and rich patrons of the arts who financed the first of the Broadway plays.

- Unlike venture capitalists, angel investors typically use their own money to fund an entrepreneurial venture they find interesting and potentially profitable at start-up. Venture capitalists, on the other hand, do not use their own money as a rule. They use institutional money from college endowments or large pension funds and they hold a fiduciary or trust responsibility to make a good investment that will earn a high rate of return. Venture capitalists are also charged with the responsibility of demanding board positions and exerting veto rights to affect the company's direction as they see fit.

- Angel investors are a bit more benign. Just like with the Broadway plays, angel investors get into a project because it appeals to them personally. That doesn't mean they don't want a nice rate of return. They certainly do and will not invest if their own financial analysis does not lead them to believe that is exactly what they will get. They are often wealthy, retired business people who look for interesting project that are too young for banks to take a chance on and for venture capitalists to be interested in. In an angel/owner relationship, you often also find a mentor/owner relationship.

Akshay too had a similar thought process and hence opted for Angel funding. Let's understand how he succeeded in achieving the funding.

"As I mentioned earlier, I got in touch with this gentleman named Mr. Anup from RCS Advisors (P) Ltd, who scouts for angel investments and he in turn got me introduced to two gentlemen who are based out of Goa with very strong financial background. These 2 gentlemen were in USA for a good time, having completed their MBA from USA and possessing a good work experience in the Silicon Valley. After they came to India, they were looking for some good platforms to invest and that is when Anup from RCS Advisors got us together. They were not those angel type angel investors nor were they my friends. They were investors who were keen to be on board for lifetime and bear the thick and thin with me, unlike professional angel investors who look for an exit after 2-5 years and hence I call them *friendly angel investors*. This is how I got my funding. They trusted on my 6 years of running around and my background and were convinced to invest in my company and also came on board with me," completes Akshay.

Interesting! A friendly angel investor, who had the necessary funds and wanted to just be a part of some upcoming and promising startup to adequately invest their funds, which eventually they did.

So how does one actually go about locating a Friendly Angel Investor?

"Well there is no set formula of locating one. It is just that one needs to be smart enough to be in the right contact, network, where you could get introduced to someone from that league. In my case, since I knew Anup from RCS Advisors, it helped me as he had someone who was keen."

So now, since it is more than a year having raised the funds, what is his take?

"Firstly, since they are more of friends than investors, there is not much pressure from their side for the recoveries. The angels, who come on board with the idea of 2-5 years of exit, put a lot of pressure on you which could prove detrimental. Here, no such thing was there as they came on board with a lifetime commitment. The pressure in question here is about everything that goes into reaping profits to get the investors their money. There is pressure of performing better; even if you are, they are constantly on your head, pushing you to limits. Then there is pressure of other kinds like minimum debts, minimum consumption of raw materials, maximum output generation, controlling labor cost, and all sorts of stuff which gets a bit exaggerated at times and hence the pressure.

Secondly, when you have professional angels on board, you feel you are employed and the fact that you own the company does not matter since your energies are all diverted to repay them. And if they have to exit in some years, they will make sure you work harder. In this aspect too, I was lucky as they did not have any plans to quit or exit from the company" says Akshay.

The exit clause mentioned here by Akshay is critical. As seen earlier, if the angel investors have a fixed exit strategy in place, the same is converted to unnecessary pressure, since they have to get their returns and leave. This will enable them to invest their profits in some other company and hence the exit is a critical thing and the entrepreneur can come under pressure in obliging the angel's exit and this brings us to some flips as well of these friendly angel investors.

Pros-
1) The friendly angels do not have the exit clause as they patiently wait for your returns to come back.
2) They give you a patient Hearing.
Cons-
1) The operational barriers that one has to face. Since they are on board, they are constantly trying to put you to challenges by opposing your thoughts and decisions, which gets troublesome.
2) One start losing confidence owing to pressure that is always mounted on you.

He goes ahead and says- "There are some flips as well and one of the major flips is the operational barriers that one has to face. Since they are on board, they are constantly trying to put you to challenges by opposing your thoughts and decisions, which gets very troublesome at times.

For preamble as a company decision, if one needs to take a diversification decision, the investors could probably take opposition. This may leave you with a kind of setback and you are really not very happy, but left without any choice, you continue to do so.

Other than owing to these kinds of situations, one starts to lose his confidence and hence it becomes important to understand that one needs to consider this as a passing phase and constantly work on his deliveries," says Akshay.

This friendly angel funding is a good bet, provided you have your vision clear. Akshay has faced many a challenge and therefore we wonder if he would recommend this method to others.

"Yes, off course, I will. There are challenges in everything that we do but it is on us how we take things. Although there will be some conditions that I request people to observe, this route to funding is good," says Akshay.

So, what are those conditions?

"A- The entrepreneur must identify the purpose of funding for which the angels are keen to invest. If their purpose is not in sync with yours, there could be several disputes arising and hence to identify the purpose is of sole importance.

B- The angel should be able to work with you and not just supervise things. He should be ready to put in his efforts as well for the desired results. This makes him all the more aware of the operational challenges and hence it is very important for him to be accustomed to the work profiles.

Last and the most important, the background of the angels must be sought with care, as if the background is not properly sought, there could be idealism differences, which may not be healthy. Moreover, a thorough background check will enable you to know the strengths and weaknesses of the angel and you are in a better position to evaluate the angel," says Akshay.

Akshay helped us to identify not only a different route of funding but has also given a holistic view of the same, thus making it simpler for us to reason out whether we would like to go for this route of funding or not.

iWeb has been applauded for their several interventions, a few glimpses of the same-iWeb Technology Solutions has graduated to the Microsoft Gold Certified Partner

Level from the Registered Partner Level. Earlier it was even a part of the Microsoft Empower Program. Gold Certified Partners have access to all tools and support from Microsoft including guaranteed telephone-based management, priority listing in the Microsoft Resource Directory and personalized one on one support on its entire range of products, technology and services.

iWeb Technology Solutions is an Advanced Business Partner of IBM and has already migrated the database to IBM DB2 Framework. iWeb has plans to migrate to IBM WebSphere middleware and get upgraded to the IBM Business Partner Premier Level to secure personalized support and joint go to market campaigns with IBM. iWeb is already running various joint go to market campaigns with IBM starting with iWeb PRM – Human Resource Module of iWeb Enterprise Suite.

Fund-O- Drama

Funding Technique – Friendly angel Investors (for Indian conditions)

Prerequisites: Good Business idea, agreement for lifetime equity by the angels, proper medium to connect to the friendly angel investors.

Time to fund	Less More
Ease of fund	Low High
Amount	Less More

6

Quick Heal

Quick Heal Technologies Pvt. Ltd. is a leading IT security solutions and an ISO 9001 certified company. Each Quick Heal product is designed to simplify IT security management across the length and depth of devices and on multiple platforms. They are customized to suit consumers, small businesses, Government establishments and corporate houses.

Over a span of 23 years, the company's R&D has focused on computer and network security solutions. The current portfolio of cloud-based security and advanced machine learning enabled solutions stop threats, attacks and malicious traffic before it strikes. This considerably reduces the system resource usage. The security solutions are indigenously developed. Quick Heal Antivirus Solutions, Quick Heal Scan Engine and the entire range of Quick Heal products are proprietary items of Quick Heal Technologies (P) Ltd. and are copyrights owned by the company.

Founder: Kailash Katkar

Kailash Katkar, the dynamic and spectacular CEO of Quick Heal is a recipient of the coveted 'GS Parkhe Industrial Merit Award 2009' awarded by MCCIA (The Mahratta Chamber of Commerce, Industries and Agriculture, a reputed body of Commerce in India). He has also been felicitated with Maxell Award for Maharashtra Corporate Excellence, 2012, in the category of Innovation by Maharashtra Chief Minister Hon'ble Shri. Prithviraj Chavan. He has also received Army Institute of Technology's (AIT) 'Young Entrepreneurs' Award. He is also the recipient of the 2012 Brands Academy Entrepreneurship Excellence Award being recognized as "Entrepreneur of the Year in IT Security ".

Kailash's strategic business partnerships have continuously produced significant business value for Quick Heal Technologies in the form of financial performance, customer satisfaction and loyalty, market share, and productivity. He also leads the strategy for how to best manage and orchestrate the delivery of Quick Heal products and services for customers. His strong commitment to operational excellence, innovative approach to business problems and aptitude for partnering cross-functionally have reshaped and leveraged the security brand as the most preferred solution in consumer and SOHO segments and have rearranged the brand preference in enterprise segment.

You have a great idea, a smart business plan, and even a good target market. It seems like the sky's the limit for what your startup company can achieve. Unfortunately, the only thing your startup lacks is capital.

Fundraising using investors can be time-consuming, tiring, and take you away from the core of your business.

Quick Heal is a name that resonates with all of us and is indeed a true brand to reckon with, seeing the robustness of its products which have made a deep impact on our minds. But have you wondered how this revolution was funded? No, it wasn't angel daddies or the banking uncles who came to Quick Heal's rescue but it was its founder Kailash Katkar's ongoing business of servicing and repairing IT gadgets, which funded it, albeit, cleverly. Yes, this is the story of Kailash Katkar, founder, Quick Heal Technologies, who used his services and repairing remuneration to fund the revolutionary and popular IT security software, Quick Heal.

"I started off as a fax machine, calculator and related IT products servicing and repairing man. The repair work for an entire year was taken care of for an annual fee. I had a small set up. However, the lingering need of going beyond the repair and maintenance service of fax machines and calculators made me think of doing something that no one catered to. Around that time, I noticed a shop in Sadashiv Peth, Pune that specialized in servicing motherboards and coincidentally there wasn't anyone who had ventured into that. Over time, I upgraded my skill to mending printers and computers. While working on a computer, I noticed that a virus was corrupting the system, and I thought what if we could resolve this. I saw a potential in this and thought this was something that could be given as a special service or a product to my clients, as in 1996, there was hardly any awareness about antivirus software," says Kailash.

He further continues "I wanted to do something in this space that wasn't explored by many, but owing to the limitations of my educational background and little knowledge in creating the software, I came to a dead end. Then one day, it struck me that my younger brother Sanjay who is a software engineer could help me and so I discussed my aspirations with him and he agreed to develop the software single handedly. After some time, he achieved success in creating the software but he wanted two more helpers to create copies of the software. Once again, I felt as if I had hit a wall. But I saw the upside to the situation and continued running the service center and thought that based on the Service center, I would request for a bank loan. I set out to apply for loans and approached a lot of banks but I was mercilessly turned down by everyone," says Kailash.

So, how did he come about to fund his own venture?

"Since I was turned down by a lot of banks, I was all but devastated and thought that I should drop the idea. And that's when something struck me. I decided to fund my venture with the aid of the service center that I was running. Now, when I thought of funding the venture through my service center, obviously that meant a lot of cost-cutting on the personal front and professional front since the service center was the only source of bread and butter for my family. To ensure that I do not end up losing out on the basic comfort of my family, I had to play safe. To take my idea ahead, I got 2 engineers to help my brother and personally took the responsibility of marketing the software", says Kailash.

It is critical when you have your P&L account of current business and are trying to translate it into a new investment, it isn't a profitable scenario. Moreover, one has to be tremendously disciplined in the way one invests the profits of existing business. It is, therefore interesting to read how Kailash managed to fund his venture and also take care of the marketing.

> When an entrepreneur decides to fund his passion through his existing business, it is a complicated situation for him. On one hand, he has to look after his family's comfort and on the other, there is always the need-based demands that your venture may pose.

Kailash says "I doubled the time I invested in my business and made it a point to take all gadgets that I could comfortably service. Further as a strategy, I cut down my costs and enlarged my service scope so that I could cater to more number of clients and more types of gadgets. Simultaneously, I started marketing the software aggressively to companies and did the same in minimum cost. I started this in 1996 and by the grace of god, by 1999, Quick Heal had started off as an independent business. I did not seek a single rupee from anyone and on the merit of my service center's revenues, I hit the bull's eye."

Wow, this was indeed an enormous feat! Kailash went all the way to nurture his knowledge of servicing gadgets. He further ensured that he could broaden the spectrum of servicing maximum gadgets so as not to lose any potential customer.

After a pause, Kailash continues,

"Unfortunately my irony did not end here and I had some bad debts that disturbed my working capital but with time and perseverance, I came out of it."

So what according to him worked in his favor through this funding?

"Yes, this funding had its own pros. To begin with, there wasn't any interest to be paid, no sword hanging on your head and what you earn is entirely yours. Secondly, there was no time wasted in preparing business presentations, impressive financial figures or other nitty-gritties to impress the bankers. Lastly, you could choose to use the revenue generated from one arm of your business, use it as and when you wish to and as per the demand of the new business. Also psychologically, since it is your own hard earned money that you are investing you are doubly cautious, which enhances your chances of playing safe."

Those were some real good merits. Quick Heal, owing to its performance, usability and robustness, has several accolades in the field of IT. Some of them are-

 *PCSL Labs: PCSL is an independent research organization focusing on security software test and test standard development. PCSL (PC Security Labs) certification is awarded to products that score 97 and above in the "PCSL Total Protection Test" held by PCSL every two months. It is one of the first tests to combine static scan test, dynamic test, static false positive test and dynamic false positive test into a single comparative test.*

Quick Heal security solutions received their first PCSL Certification in July 2010 for Quick Heal Total Security 2009. The product received a five star certification as the best antivirus.

Deloitte.
Technology Fast50
India 2010 winner
Quick Heal Technologies is amongst the Deloitte Technology's Fast 50, India 2010 list. The Technology Fast 50 India Program is conducted by Deloitte Touche Tohmatsu. It is a ranking of India's 50 fastest growing and most dynamic technology companies based on percentage revenue growth over the past three years.

Quick Heal Technologies was ranked 16ᵗʰ on the list with phenomenal growth of 244% in last three years.

Spectacular! The risk, which Kailash took for funding Quick Heal through his service center, did turn the tables for him. But since it is your one hand holding the other, there could be some challenges as well.

Kailash says, "Yes, there are some limitations, rather they are challenges or risks that you should be prepared to face:

A - The funds would be limited if your enterprise is not big enough, thus putting a lot of restrictions on your plans. Your plan to grow your startup phase-wise could be hampered since the periodical pumping of money could be hampered. Moreover, sometimes the working capital of your existing business from where you are funding could go out of cycle, thus resulting in some debts for you.

B-One needs to be on a shoestring budget on a personal and professional level. That implies sacrificing a lot of luxuries in personal life and working in a very structured and thought about process in the professional life, taking utmost care that you do not swerve from your goal".

Oops! Those indeed could be some risks that may digress you from your goals.

But with some perseverance and smart work, the ball can keep rolling till you realize your ultimate dream, as in the case of Kailash.

Any further guru gyan (Some Knowledge sharing) from Kailash?

"This is a stringent way of funding your dream, but if one can hold on and be patient, it does pay. I held on to my dream for 3 years and worked hard on it and finally the new venture was independent and is today a leading IT security software not only in India but internationally in almost 60 countries says Kailash.

That is important. As mentioned earlier, a little patience, smart work and perseverance can lead you to your goal. So what does Kailash feel? Will he ever take this route for funding again?

"For sure, Although I may not need to do it again, as in 2010, I was fortunate enough to receive a funding of USD 600 million. But yes, if need arises, I will do it again," says Kailash.

Quick Heal today, as we all know, is a leading IT security software with the company having a turnover of over USD 3 billion. Quick Heal has also been instrumental in acquiring the leading technological company Apoorva Technologies, which speaks volumes of Quick Heal's success and that too from a modest source of funding, who could have thought? Amazing!

Technology Partners of Quick Heal:

 Microsoft is a leading manufacturer of Operating Systems, System Software and Application Software. Quick Heal is a Microsoft Gold Certified Partner, and this partnership gives Quick Heal an opportunity to build a close working relationship with Microsoft, allowing Quick Heal to deliver quality products and technology solutions built for Microsoft platform.

 Intel®, the world leader in silicon innovation, develops technologies, products and initiatives to continually advance how people work and live. Quick Heal is an Intel Software Partner and its products are optimized for Intel architecture.

Fund-O- Drama

Funding Technique – Funding from your other ongoing business.

Prerequisites: Reasonable earnings from ongoing business, calculated risk analysis and patience.

Time to fund	Less More
Ease of fund	Low High
Amount	Less More

7

Ms. Veena Gundavelli,

Women empowerment is something we all live by, understand and want it to be realized today. But how about a time when this was not as rampant as it is today and that too in a place where seeing a woman stand up for her Entrepreneurial passion and seeking VC funding was more conspicuous and almost unheard of.

Yes, I am talking about one such woman, Ms. Veena Gundavelli who obtained her multimillion-dollar funding in the late 90's for her then emerging and now highly successful company, Emagia.

Emagia, today is one of the leading companies in Silicon Valley which is into the business of helping customers consolidate Order-to-Cash information on a single platform and enhance control on daily operations pertaining to all aspects of receivables management.

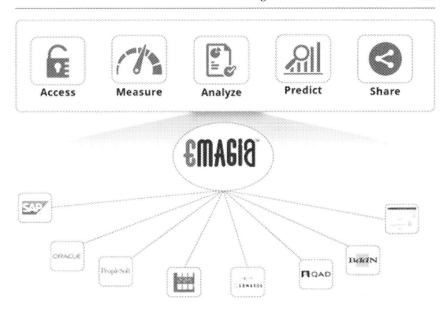

Emagia Order-to-Cash Analytics solution brings the power of business intelligence with ease-of-use self-service visualizations and prepackaged integrations with leading financial systems. Finance executives can gain powerful insight without depending on IT and without dealing with lengthy and costly business intelligence implementations.

Born and raised in Hyderabad, India, Veena completed her engineering in Electronics and Communication from Osmania University and her Master's in Computer Engineering from Santa Clara University in 1990.

"When I came here in the 1990's, there were only vegetable farms all around. There were a lot of fruit orchards as well and this place was completely different back then" remembers Veena and continues,

"There used to be only one Indian restaurant back then called *Pasand* and we would be so excited to be there as that would bring back sweet memories of India for us."

Well, yes, many things since then have changed and Veena gets nostalgic thinking about those times.

So how did Veena embark on this journey of leading a multimillion-dollar company in the valley?

"As I was completing my Masters, I joined Cannon in their Printers division. We were the first team of people who worked on the concept of Color bubble jet printer. It was a novelty back then. I would work on the algorithms to match the color technology. It was a mind-blowing experience and I got to learn a lot."

That is a fascinating work profile indeed – working on new inventions and technologies yet to be introduced to the world. There is another interesting thing to note. Veena was completing her education and working full-time. How did she manage it?

"Being a woman, I knew if I had to fulfill my passion, I had to stretch and work on the lines of commitment, dedication and adventure. I was fortunate that Cannon took care of my fees at the college and I could work and study both. It was tiring at times, but it was very satisfying as it would give me a lot of happiness and immense learning."

That is a true sign of an Entrepreneur and it does bring out the best in you when you are resolute. Veena was sure of her career goals and what she wanted to achieve in life. Furthermore, sheer determination, strong will and focus propelled her towards achieving those very set goals.

Post her stint with Cannon, Veena joined Cisco, working on the networking side. This was a rejuvenating experience for her and added to her skill set that she was acquiring at a fast pace.

In 1989 Veena tied the knot with Mr. Sai and moved to the USA. Mr. Sai has been in the US since 1986 and is the founder and CEO of Solix Technologies, who was also parallelly working on his company. However, Veena in 1998 decided to branch out on her own and her passion led to the founding of her company - Solix Internet Technologies, an expense management system company.

Everything was going well until her then smooth sailing ship hit an Iceberg.

"In 2000 there was a massive crash of the markets and lot of people had to declare bankruptcy. It was a tough time and the only good that happened with us then was that we could sail through and emerge as winners. But we had to change some things and align ourselves to the market conditions," says Veena.

They were quick enough to realize the need for change and the ongoing market scenarios and their own platform building skills compelled them to reboot the company; making it bigger and better and hence the birth of Emagia. Emagia, founded in 2003 is a company that focuses on Accounts Receivable, Automation and Credit to Customer.

"We wanted to have tools in place for large corporations who have shared services centers and help companies collect their money faster. It was an automation tool helping them track all their transactions," says Veena.

Veena had already faced a jolt with the dot com crash in the year 2000 and hence she wanted to consolidate her foundation first before she sought funding and hence began by first investing her own savings into the business. She and her husband funded the company in its nascent years.

"For a product company, you need funding, do a lot of branding, stand with 6-12 months of selling cycle, deploy people and much more and that is where all our money went. We had to first build the foundation and that paid off as we were successful in making it sustainable and then pitch ourselves to the VC bench," says Veena and continues, "For VC funding and for seeking that large chunk of money, we were sure we will need to make ourselves financially viable. So, we started to visit a lot of TiE chapters, building on network and trying to gain some validation by large corporations to get the real value of our products out in the market."

Veena was focused and knew that soon she would have to have her VC funding in place, and she was smart and understood that in order to receive the funding the company's status would need to elevated enough to be termed 'bankable'. Her fortitude paid off and one of the most reputed corporations - Tyco (now merged with Johnson Controls) gave them their first big order.

"It was dreamlike and ecstatic a feeling to have finally bagged that order and it did go on to prove that our product did carry some value. And that was also the time, that we were ready to get our VC funding in place and then began my next set of adventure," laughs Veena while reminiscing.

Seeking VC funding at that time for a company in Silicon Valley, that too by a woman, was unusual to say the least. Things were not as streamlined, social media was not prevalent, experiences were few to share, and of course the environment was not very conducive. Despite all this, Veena was determined to make it big.

Emagia was fortunate and they got another big validation from the giant Solectron, now called Flextronics. That was another good jump for them, but that was not going to be the end of her story and she says, "I started to confidently pitch my proposals to many VC's, and I used to be rejected by everyone. The apprehensions that most of them would have is, being a woman, would I be able to scale up things, and being from India, will I be able to manage and make things happen here? Will the scalability be there?"

Today, in all probability these questions may never arise. But 15 years ago, these were valid apprehensions that existed. But a lot has changed since then and Veena did succeed in procuring her first round of funding by a VC.

Remembering, Veena says, "Oh, that was so rewarding, and all the years of hard work paid off and there began my second phase of journey where I had to ensure that I justify the VC funding. I got my funding in 3 different rounds with a gap of one year each between them."

So, how was it like? Did they have harsh conditions or how was it, overall?

"It was good, they did see my passion and will to succeed as crucial must haves. But they also wanted me to bring on board a sales-oriented CEO, which was fine since I too wanted to partner with someone from sales. This would help the company achieve new highs in sales and that would give me the opportunity to now focus on other crucial parts of business," says Veena and continues "They also brought a team with them and took a little higher a stake compared to the founders. That was fine but what really was not very fine was the inexperience of people who came on board with the VC's and that inexperience burnt down a lot of company cash."

When you are riding with so much money, everything that you do matters a lot and here specifically, since it was the team from VC, things should have been more professional but that did not happen and the prospects of the company took a beating.

"Obviously we were not the ones to lose hope and we rebooted the company once again with our own funds and customer funding and that again brought us back on track and things were back to where they were" beams Veena.

It is said 'where there's a will, there is a way' and Veena did have her will in place. She not only ensured that she utilized the VC funding properly, but also scaled up her company well. Today Emagia carries a name for itself and with the introduction of her latest product, the digital finance assistant 'Gia', Emagia is on a roll. [both roll and high imply the same thing]

Supercharge Your Finance Operations

So, after receiving this VC funding in an era where it was not very common, that too for a woman, how does she feel about it and would she ever repeat it?

"Of course, I would. Now, times are different. Back then, when I would be sitting there waiting for my turn to pitch, and in almost all scenarios, I would be the only woman there.

Veena had her challenges, and she lists below the pros and cons –

Advantages -

1) Having a VC fund is obviously a good validation for your products and services and in my case there were 3 VC's who funded me so, all the better for a validation if you are seeking one.

2) It's a validation not only for my company but also for what I offer and this boosts the demand in the market for products and services on offer.

3) It is a good learning to see how the VC funders really think and evaluate your proposals. The same, for sure, teaches you a lot.

Disadvantages -

1) Be prepared for performance and that now onwards, you have the pressure to prove yourself even more.

2) The VC from whom you are seeking your funds should understand your business and should work with you diligently on it. But that does not happen very often and hence puts a lot of pressure on you to perform.

3) Typically, VC's expect miracles, therefore, the hockey stick revenue model to unfold. This is not true however and hence it becomes a point of altercation most of the times.

Veena has been candid about her experiences and says further, "One must understand his/her own space and product, build the right connections and take it from there. That matters a lot."

So, what advice would she want to give the new entrepreneurs who carry the passion and determination to be torch bearers one day?

"Build good mentor network, get advice of people in similar space and do your homework well. Do not follow a trend just for the sake of it or because others are doing it. Do it only if you understand it and can master it. Also, always remember, if you can go with smaller VC's. Get yourself attuned to their requirements, working styles and then jump for the real vultures, else you may end up beaten up."

Well this surely is one piece of advice to take home and Venna reiterates the fact that nothing is impossible. As Walt Disney once said, "If you can dream it, you can do it," and Veena has proved that.

Well I am grateful and happy that I could interview this woman of substance, and as I plan to wrap up, I am requested for a last byte from Veena and she says, "You know what Mehul, I need to say this one thing - Women Entrepreneurs are docile and are not taught to be the trail blazers. They are always asked to stay in limits, not do certain things and that results in them getting to avail of exposure very late in their lives. This is unfair to them. They also deserve to be given equal weightage and importance and then you see, how they will emerge as the winners and great influencers of this universe."

That is so true Veena and I agree to that. Women today are already powerful and with a little shift in our mindsets, they can do even better. That was the great story of one of the leading Woman CEO's of the Silicon Valley and it was amazing to have spoken to her.

Fund-O- Drama

Funding Technique – **Funding through multiple VC's**

Prerequisites: Own capital, robust business plan, good validation from big customers, plan of growth in place.

Time to fund	
	Less More
Ease of fund	
	Low High
Amount	
	Less More

8

Chumbak

Founder: Shubhra Chaddha

'Chumbak' designs and manufactures products in the form of Magnets (Chumbak means Magnets) and hence the name. Today they have over 30 categories of products including fridge magnets, keychains, bobble heads, t-shirts and boxer shorts, coffee mugs, phone cases, laptop sleeves and a whole bunch more! And to think, there is a lot more from where that came from!

Meet Shubhra Chadda, the Founder of Chumbak, who was a quintessential girl next door, and who, like millions of us, completed her studies and got into the 'Big Daddy's', corporate world only to get struck with this awesome idea and finally surrendering to her passion of magnets, starting right from conceptualizing, designing and selling it and making it big in this arena. Chadda graduated in travel and tourism from Mount Carmel College, Bengaluru in 2000 but, due to limited opportunities then, went on to work in finance and later marketing with 'KPMG' and 'Nortel' respectively.

Shubhra and her husband Vivek who later joined 'Chumbak' loved to travel all over and that's how the concept was formed. Each time they travelled, they would shop for souvenirs, especially fridge magnets. Being on really small budgets, fridge magnets made amazing and affordable gifts to friends and family back home. For some strange reason, they could never find fun fridge magnets right here in India. So in 2004, they started doing some initial research but weren't able to get anywhere. Finally in

2009, they got their act together and spent a good six months on researching various products. They narrowed down to a bunch of fun things that they did have and also those that they loved to buy and use.

"When I started Chumbak, I used the money from my savings and my Provident Fund and got my first line up of magnet products ready and, after the lot got ready, I showed it to a lot of retailers and wholesalers, who loved it and they encouraged me to take the next obvious step of full-fledged going ahead with its manufacturing. That was the time when I was at crossroads, not knowing where to go. On one hand, I had the promising potential of my concept and on other hand, I had scarcity of liquid funds and that is when I decided to sell my ONLY house!!!" says Shubra.

"Pardon me; did you actually sell your only house? Who sells a house to fund one's venture?" This was my reaction to Shubra when she told me that she actually sold her ONLY house to fund her venture.

Yes, you might say Shubra went maybe a bit crazy and decided to make money for her dreams by selling the only roof over her head. Chumbak's twitter profile (https://twitter.com/Chumbak) says that they are a little mad and maybe we should attribute the same madness to her. In India, a country where selling your house is sacrilegious and only next to disposing your family gold and silver, Shubra was bold enough to take this inevitable step to fuel her passion.

Was it that easy? Generally one witnesses stereotyped family dramas with parents, relatives and friends opposing and in her case it could also be the husband playing the wicked witch of not letting it happen … so I wonder what she did for this and the first thing that strikes my mind is that she must have had some thoughts to herself about the frightening outcomes that her decision of selling her house could have had. Didn't Shubra have any qualms about it? Shubra smiles and says-

"Yes, I was a little hesitant, what if I would have been unable to sustain my business and would have had to look out for some obligation from my parents or my friends or relatives to stay with them till we could again recover our losses and this very thought was nightmarish. Whenever I used to think of this, it would give me goose bumps and I would go weak in my knees thinking if this decision was right or not. But I finally decided that I need to do it and whatever happens, I will fight it out and so I continued my passion for 'Chumbak' and took this turning point decision of my life," says Shubra.

That's great but even after Shubra made her decision she could have had some opposition from her parents or husband, Vivek, as mentioned above. What was their stand? Didn't they oppose her, to which she retorts -

"No, I had no interference from my parents or in-laws or Vivek, as Vivek and me had bought this flat on our own money and hence it was solely our decision and it was difficult for us to sell as we were very attached to the house, considering the fact that we did a lot of foot work for it right from deciding on the colors of the walls, the interior designing, the showpieces that we bought. It was all our hard work and to just give it away was really disastrous for us but Vivek supported me." Here she becomes a little poignant but continues further, "but it was all for good reasons, so I am happy and Vivek aptly supported me," smiles Shubra. He not only supported her then but later joined her full time to make Chumbak a multimillion-dollar company, which went on to get funded from Seed fund, the same fund which has invested in Carwale and Red Bus.

Wasn't mortgaging the house an option? "Yes it was," says Shubhra, "but I did not want the sword of interest hanging on my head every moment. I was without a house but at least I did not have a bloodhound sniffing at my doorstep every month." She raises an interesting thought. Is it better to mortgage your house or sell it if that is the way you have decided to raise funds? Before you judge mortgaging the house as an obvious winner, consider the following points -

The Interest outflow will always be significantly more than the rental outflow. So in a way you are depleting your capital more every month.

The amount you will get for mortgaging your house will be only 60-70% of the value of the house. So instead of the 40 lakhs which Shubhra was able to collect, she would have got about 25 lakhs in loans.

If your venture fails, in both cases, the end result will be the same - you will lose your house.

So maybe Shubhra's decision to sell her house is not so foolish after all. The possible downside to selling your house quickly is that you might get a lower than expected value.

"Yes, there was a little haste but not so much that would have affected my price drastically, so more or less, I got a good deal," says Shubra.

Was it also difficult for Shubhra to shift her house to a temporary place, after all, she had the liability of making the shifting expenses, the ruckus to get her organized in a make shift apartment, so was not this a huge burden on her?

Shubhra candidly replies, "Not really as our focus was on our goal. Yes, there were challenges but we all took it in our stride and managed the show. We did not want to? dilute the goal that we envisaged and hence it really did not matter".

This reminds me of an interesting anecdote of yet another dare devil and a genius entrepreneur Raunaq Singh, founder of the 7th largest tyre manufacturing company in the world-The Apollo Tyres. Today, Raunaq Group comprises of Raunaq international ltd, Bharat Steel Tubes Ltd., Apollo Tyres Ltd, Menarini Raunaq Pharma Limited, Bharat Gears ltd and many more companies.

Raunaq Singh was born on August 16 in the year 1922 to a middle class family in Daska, now Pakistan. In 1947, India became independent from the clutches of the British. Post-independence, British India was divided into two independent countries, India and Pakistan, in order to settle the religious conflicts between the Hindus and the Muslims. Like many other non-Muslims living in Pakistan, Raunaq Singh also had a very hard time surviving in Pakistan. So, he moved to India as a refugee in 1947.

Raunaq Singh moved to India as a refugee from Pakistan, in 1947. He, along with 13 others, camped out in a small one room apartment in Gole Market, Delhi. Raunaq Singh worked on a small spice shop in the neighborhood, Munilal Bajaj & Co. so as to make ends meet. The job gave him an income of 1 paisa a day, which was just not enough to keep the family going.

His finances were the only thing holding him back from starting his own venture. Thus, in November, 1947, he decided to sell off his wife's jewellery in Delhi's old Chandni Chowk Market for a sum of eight thousand Indian rupees (115 USD Approx) to head to Kolkata to test his luck.

In Kolkata, Raunaq Singh opened his first spice trade shop at 85, Netaji Subhash road. The venture was successful and he was able to make a decent living. But, his destiny was about to change. Soon, he set up Bharat Steel Pipes ltd., which later established itself as the biggest steel pipe manufacturing company in the Indian history.

Phew! What a dynamic entrepreneur. Someone has rightly put "luck and fortune, favors the brave" which was evident in the case of Raunaq Singh and now in case of Shubhra also.

But yes, it still sounds a bit crazy to me, so I asked Shubhra if she would do this again if she had to fund another venture? "I will but the next time, I will be a little careful as in I will take some financial advice from an expert to guide me appropriately. It was a big risk I took which fortunately worked in my favor but yes, if required I will definitely do it again."

> "I will also recommend this method to all others very strongly but will also put in a word of caution to analyze the financials of it and the possible effects completely.

<u>The Chumbak Studio</u>

They started by out working at home. Like most startups, they worked and lived in the same place, enjoying the fun of working in boxer shorts. They had work meetings at home, where suddenly you'd be talking to a partner about something really important. They progressed and started off at a 1000 sqft with 7 people and then they outgrew that and asked the landlord to build 2 floors above them. This was home till 4 months ago :) Today they work out of The 'Chumbak' Studio. It's an integrated office and warehouse. It took them 5 months to build and they are quite thrilled with the huge space that they have.

Wow… what wisdom. Hope you guys don't set out immediately to sell off your bricks but smartly weigh the proposal and think and then proceed. Our fund-o- drama will further help you to take a constructive call.

The rest of her story is delightful to hear -

Shubha turned Magnets, which seems like a very trivial thing into a multimillion dollar business. Today, other than its mainstay of fridge magnets, Chumbak also sells quirky designer t-shirts, boxer shorts, iPhone cases, coin pouches, bags, keychains, charms, laptop sleeves, phone covers, USB keys, notebooks, mousepads, bookmarks, wrapping paper, coffee mugs, coasters and shot glasses. Towards the end of 2012, Seed

Fund (Mahesh Murthy and Praveen Gandhi) funded 'Chumbak' for an undisclosed amount. Finally, she has enough money to take her company to the next level.

Fund-O- Drama

Funding Technique – **Selling your only house and shifting to a rented house.**

Prerequisites: A house with value matching your requirement, some kind of initial thing going on so that you have confidence, getting buy in from the family, having the courage to shift to a rented place

Time to fund	
	Less More
Ease of fund	
	Low High
Amount	
	Less More

9

STROMBSS

Vihaan Natural Health Care (P) Ltd is a leading trader, supplier and manufacturer of health foods, nutrition foods, health shakes, protein shakes, women's food, breakfast cereals, whole grains and many more. It has its popular brand called STROMBSS which has become very known with the masses.

STROMBSS is an idea that germinated out of a mother's need to supplement her children's diet with natural nutritious food. Kids today are so overwhelmed with options of tasty but unhealthy foods that they refuse to have the dals, sprouts, whole grains and vegetables willingly. Even whole grain bread does not appeal to adults as much as plain white or brown bread.

Founder: Priya Parab

Priya is a B.com (Bachelor in Commerce) and MBA from Mumbai University and has15 years of rich corporate multi-industry experience in manufacturing, hospitality, media, banking and international freight in companies like Bennett and Coleman, UTI Bank Ltd, plus 5 years as an entrepreneur. Besides sales and marketing that is her core expertise, she also has proficiency in startups, projects, systems and operations. Currently, she is following her passion of reaching STROMBSS to the health-aware global consumer. She endeavors to better the nutrition quotient of not only the over-nourished but the under-nourished as well.

Many avenues have opened up these days for the budding entrepreneurs to fund themselves. Some of them opt for the more complexed modes of funding whilst few go for the years old method of getting funded.

Priya's story is one such story as she had the time-honored way of financing her startup through a term loan and cash credit limit which she took. Although this kind of funding may seem to look as an ordinary one, but friends, there is a lot that this mode of funding can do.

Priya explains her funding story-

"After my product was established, I decided to fund my unit and hence started running pillar to post with my documents to seek bank loan. A year passed by and I was not entertained anywhere for my loan. Since I had no history of great financials, I was turned down at every step. The other thing that was an obstacle was my requirement which was only USD 2 Million. The banks did not find much scope in my proposal as they would not entertain loans below USD 10 Million. Despite of showing them the promise my products had in the market, none of the banks actually agreed to fund me," says Priya.

Sometimes funding requirements also pose challenges to an entrepreneur as in the case of Priya. Her requirement, however small, was a requirement which, should get funded and it did. So how did the turnaround actually come about?

The turnaround of funding-

"Amidst my struggle to run around from bank to bank trying to convince them to fund me, I got in touch with a gentleman who suggested me to go to the SBI (State Bank of India) headquarters in BKC, Mumbai and put up my case. I therefore got in touch with a senior person in SBI (State Bank of India) in Mumbai. I put up my proposal to them and explained to them what vision or path I was to tread with the loan and after much negotiations and convincing them, I finally got my bank loan in the form of a term loan and a cash credit limit. It was in July, 2011 when I finally succeeded in availing the loan," says Priya with a sigh.

It did take Priya some negotiation skills to convince the twisted bank officials to get herself funded. But once she succeeded at her gust, she was granted the term loan.

let's first understand what is exactly meant by a term loan and a cash credit-

A term loan is a monetary loan that is repaid in regular payments over a set period of time. Term loans usually last between one and ten years but may last as long as 30 years in some cases. A term loan usually involves an unfixed interest rate that will add additional balance to be repaid.

A cash credit (also popularly called as CC Limit) is a short-term cash loan to a company. A bank provides this type of funding only when the required security is given to secure the loan. Once a security for repayment has been given, the business that receives the loan can continuously draw from the bank up to a certain specified amount. This kind of facility is generally extended to businesses to manage their working capital requirements. This cash credit account is similar to a current account and also calls for a cheque book issued with it.

For Cash credit, the purpose for which loan is required is essential to ascertain, as for different purposes different types of loan can be taken. In Priya's case the loan was required to purchase fixed assets like plant and machinery. Term loan must be taken as plant and machinery are long term assets and it will take time in repayment of the loan that can be done in EMI's (Equated Monthly Installments). For working capital needs, a long term loan is not required as repayment does not require long period, hence cash credit may be availed.

As a combination of these two kinds of loans, Priya managed her funds as she had intended.

So what was the deal that was cracked by Priya and the bank-?

"I got a year of moratorium although it was to be 6 months but somehow, I could manage to convince them for 1 year of moratorium. Rest, I did not have to offer any collateral as I had my plant and machinery which was pledged against my term loan, says Priya.

As mentioned above, her term loan was there for the purchase of plant and machinery with a bonus which was that she did not have to pledge collaterals for her term loan as she availed of the CGTSME (Credit Guarantee Fund Trust for Micro and Small Enterprises) scheme of SIDBI wherein SIDBI provides the third party collateral on her behalf to the bank and the association of CC limit took care of her working capital.

SIDBI pleading for her? Wow! This sounds something interesting! So what is this CGTSME scheme?

Availability of bank credit without the hassles of collaterals / third party guarantees would be a major source of support to the first generation entrepreneurs to realize their dream of setting up a unit of their own Micro and Small Enterprise (MSE). Keeping this objective in view, Ministry of Micro, Small & Medium Enterprises (MSME), Government of India launched Credit Guarantee Scheme (CGS) so as to strengthen credit delivery system and facilitate flow of credit to the MSE sector.

To operationalize the scheme, Government of India and SIDBI set up the Credit Guarantee Fund Trust for Micro and Small Enterprises (CGTMSE).

The main objective is that the lender should give importance to project viability and secure the credit facility purely on the primary security of the assets financed. The other objective is that the lender availing guarantee facility should endeavor to give composite credit to the borrowers so that the borrowers obtain both term loan and working capital facilities from a single agency. The Credit Guarantee scheme (CGS) seeks to reassure the lender that, in the event an MSE unit, which availed collateral free credit facilities, fails to discharge its liabilities to the lender, the Guarantee Trust would make good the loss incurred by the lender up to 75 / 80/ 85 per cent of the credit facility.

In this case typically, a big waiver could be freedom from putting your house/shop or any other infrastructure as security. This could block your property and shy you off from any other opportunities pertaining to property until the loan is repaid.

On the other hand, Moratorium is an interesting part of the loan availed from the bank. It entitles you to additional time to pay your debt. This is a special incentive offered by banks as in the case of Priya which was 1 year.

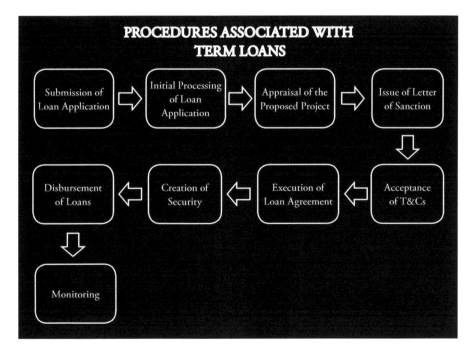

PROCEDURES ASSOCIATED WITH TERM LOANS

Submission of Loan Application → Initial Processing of Loan Application → Appraisal of the Proposed Project → Issue of Letter of Sanction

Disbursement of Loans ← Creation of Security ← Execution of Loan Agreement ← Acceptance of T&Cs

Monitoring

After finally getting the loan sanctioned and seeing my manufacturing unit being set up, I was very happy and also realized a few merits of this form of funding-

A, since it is a capital intensive and FMCG project, the bank loan seems to be the cheapest option available as it is not very cumbersome to pay a bank loan relatively as compared to offering equity to your investor.

B, without having much to offer (in her case, only the plant and machinery) I got the loan and hence the repayment or may be the output as the cost of money is not much," says Priya.

In the same breath and also on a compromiser note, she mentions the demerits of the same-

"Yes I have also had to see, rather am seeing, a lot of demerits.

One, to get the loan sanctioned is a tough job. It took me more than a year to get the same sanctioned. Then there are these whole lots of documents that are required to get the loan going.

Two, the monthly EMI's are a tough nut to manage as you need to make month on month provisions for them, thus it could affect your working capital cycle as sometimes you may want to focus your funds on more of resources than the outputs.

Three, you cannot skip even one installment as otherwise the banks could blacklist you. Moreover, the credit history of one gets disturbed which could prove detrimental for your future loans that you would like to seek," says Priya.

The combination of the term loan and CC limit which Priya opted for, not only got her plans floating but also her conviction in the kind of loan and so Priya, the boisterous, lively, lady after experiencing this kind of funding for 2 whole years, is keen to repeat this source of funding but also heeds a valuable piece of advice whilst recommending the same to other potential startups-

"Since I was a newbie to all of this, I missed calculating a lot of minor costs in my project cost, which unfortunately made my project cost very cut to cut. A slight deduction of finances from the bank while sanctioning my loan created a lot of stir for me, which became a huge challenge to manage. Therefore one must envisage all possible costs and keep some margins for any corner cutting by banks.

Secondly one must have the arrangement of own margins to the tune of 25% at least of the total required funds. In my case, I had to shell out 50 % of margin money as my project cost was very cut to cut and it took a year for my plant and machinery to get commissioned after sanctioning of loan. Thus had to bear the brunt of interest I was paying. If you avoid the mistake I did in estimating my project cost, a minimum of 25% arrangement at your end is strongly advised.

Lastly, keep an account of your margin money of how and where you spent it as that will enable you to show it to the bank that you are credit worthy as you have spent from your pocket the maximum you could, thus improving chances of having a good ratio of bank loan from the bank," says Priya.

"As all mothers, I too was always concerned for the right food for my children and I thought that there should be something which is tasty, yet nutritious and also affordable to bang on and hence the idea of Strombss struck me. I put in my savings from pocket and started developing food samples of my products. I then started distributing those food samples free of cost as part of test marketing to know where my products stand and this is how I started rolling out my geniuses from the stable," says Priya.

Wow, Priya has indeed fought her way out and has emerged a winner in doing what she does best, produce nutritious food. Priya intervenes me and cautions of the following conditions-

"I think if you are not educated enough to avail these loans or have less awareness about it, I suggest please seek professional help; else you may lose out on the proper deal in the long run and end up paying more. You can always negotiate the professional charges and accordingly seek the necessary help.

Secondly, there are government subsidies offered to certain segments of businesses like food industry, and I was not aware about it in my case. Now after I have got my loan sanctioned, I am trying to seek the subsidy. Hence, please be aware of the subsidies that could be there for your line of business and if you are eligible you must try for the same while getting your loan sanctioned, as this will help reduce your loan burden," completes Priya.

Incredible, this is a story of valor, determination and honest confessions of the mistakes that an entrepreneur could make while seeking this kind of funding and I am sure you will definitely learn a thing or two from Priya's daredevil attempt of availing this source of funding.

Strombss is committed to bring together nature and technology to provide natural and nutritious products of the highest quality, in easy-to-consume forms to the discerning, health conscious and fast-paced consumers of today. Their mission is also to reach out to the less privileged and educate and help them in meeting their daily nutritional needs and do their bit at preventing deaths from malnutrition.

It's their constant endeavor to bring to you natural, delicious and nutritious food for which they also look forward to your ideas and contributions.

Catch a glimpse of the Strombss factory on CNBC- log on to

-TV18 http://bit.ly/13xWi0v

Natural nutrition for 2-12-year olds

Sugar-less mini meals for diabetics

Fund-O- Drama

Funding Technique – **A structured term loan and cash credit limit from a banking institution**

Prerequisites - A good and established product line, capital intensive project, robust business plan and adequate margin money as your contribution.

Time to fund	▢▢ Less More
Ease of fund	▢▢▢ Low High
Amount	▢▢▢ Less More

10

Happily Unmarried

Happily Unmarried was established in 2003 to make fun products, do music festivals, work with Corporate and lately they have been doing a lot of projects involving branding, communication, interiors and marketing all rolled into one. Happily unmarried is the company that manufactures quirky, funky products. They are into fun gifts and lifestyle accessories. They make products which make people smile and they have a lot of fun making them.

Founder: Rajat Tuli

Meet Rajat Tuli, Co-founder of Happily Unmarried, the company that is creating news in lifestyle products, gifts and accessories markets with its desi designs. His friend Mr. Rahul Anand too was a founder to this startup.

Rajat and Rahul are graduates from the prestigious Mudra Institute of Communications, Ahmedabad in India. Rajat and Rahul worked for different ad agencies for four years. In 2003, Rajat joined a software firm, which went bankrupt and then he and one of his friends decided it was time to start their own enterprise. They realized that there were hardly any brands dedicated to India's pop-culture and youth.

Their former employers had not paid them for the last six months and they had no capital to get their venture off the ground. Pawning a laptop given to them by their old company raised 25,000 Indian rupees (Approx 360 USD)which was not even enough for them to hire office space and they operated they out of cyber cafes for the first couple of years.

To offer you a glimpse, one of their early products was an ashtray, which was a replica of traditional dhobi iron and they started with the model p and then the Bottle Lamps representing various Indian states, with localized tag lines.

Since the USD 300 managed by his savings was not a great idea, Rajat cracked up the idea of getting funded through his friends. He had limited choices and out of the ones available, he did crack the whip and laid out a plan to make his friends his savior.

"Hey do you trust me, if yes, I can give you a proposition"

This is what Rajat asked his friends before he was funded by 8 of them for his venture "Happily Unmarried" based out of Delhi, India.

Money from friends, I mean really?? What's so new in that?? I mean don't we all, day in and day out, keep taking small loans from our friends in the pretext that we will pay them later, which we may not pay eventually, and therefore it is such a casual thing to do that sometimes we don't even remember about it.

The friends and family round is critical in the life cycle of the new enterprise. At a time when few, if any, outside parties are ready to invest, sign contracts or enter into sales and marketing deals with a brand-new company that has no customers and no sales, family and close associates of the entrepreneur, pool their financial resources and rally around the individual they've known for a long time and who they trust to "be smart with and spend wisely" the funds they provide. This "insider" round is further typified by smaller increments per investor, when compared to the second round of more formal "outside" capital.

Rajat has made this so obvious and simply looking thing an innovative way of getting his start up funded. He very cleverly overcomes the initial hiccup of this rigorous process of a startup funding.

As per Mr. David Newton, a professor of entrepreneurial finance and head of the entrepreneurship program, which he founded in 1990, at Westmont College in Santa Barbara, California, the first round (also known as the "A" round) is generally considered the time to raise capital from friends and family. It's interesting to note that these investors put their money in perhaps the most risky point in the life of the venture. Unlike the subsequent—and more formal—"B" round, the firm probably has little or no revenue, few, if any, units sold or contracts signed, is probably still in the process of making any joint marketing deals, has yet to complete a successful test of its manufacturing infrastructure, and has not closed any sales agreements or been granted any product development rights or patents. These investors will say things like, "At this early stage, I'm not so much investing in the horse as I am in the jockey." They are backing the individual with the ideas, passion and vision to make this new enterprise a reality.

So how did Rajat actually go about it?

"I was working with a company before I started this venture and since the company was going through rough times, we were not paid our salaries on time and that created a lot of unpleasantness in me and one day I thought of this idea of having my own venture, but the challenge was funds, so I did the unexpected. I borrowed USD 300 $ from market by mortgaging my laptop that my company had given me," says Rajat whose first funding source was as fastidious as this one.

The company laptop on mortgage to get your dreams going, my goodness; but hold on, that is not what we are talking about here, it is much more interesting for the way he went about raising his initial capital for his venture.

Innovative business concept and hence innovative funding source as well. Funding from his friends!

Who knows you and your passion, your startup better than those in your life? With just a simple business plan to help explain your vision, you'd be surprised how eager friends and family can be to support your success. Their contribution can range from giving you money to contributing their time and effort (this can range from specialized skills like programming to simply driving across town to pick up supplies for the office).

Like all of us, Rajat too had a group of friends, the buddies, the 2 am friends, with whom we cherish our best moments.

"I decided to tap my friends as my partners in making my venture roll with the initial capital that was required," says Rajat.

When Rajat moved around meeting his friends asking them for the funds, he had a mixed reception from his friends. some just stared at him thinking is he serious?? while some played the role of a grand ma by extending their piece of advice bogging him down saying that he should not risk doing his own business, etc, etc which was not required then. But there was light at the end of the tunnel to beckon Rajat with his dreams. Some of his friends became sponsors for him and turned out to be the much needed *angel friends* who funded him.

So did Rajat face any difficulty in convincing his friends who funded him?

Rajat immediately responds-"Not really! Although it did take some time for them to understand the concept but largely it was their faith on me that enabled them to fund me, coupled with the brilliant business concept I had in my mind."

I am sure you must be thinking that ok fine he got funded from his friends, but why so many of them, couldn't one of his friends, fund his entire capital?

The answer is simple, which holds a simple strategy, which is worth noting here and that is don't keep all your eggs in one basket but divide the risk amongst all. Rajat too did not want to have one friend hovering over him for a big chunk of money and hence had petty contributions from multiple friends, thus dividing his risk.

A second school of thought to this strategy also was that had he offered one person the stake, the equity that he would have had to offer would have been much more as that one person's demands could be higher considering that he was solely putting in equity.

Fine, so you have many friends or more than one friend pitching in the money for you. Would this source of funding call for any advantages?

"There could be many advantages to the funding source of friends…" says Rajat which gets me inquisitive and I further probe him to tell me those.

"Well, firstly there is no need to be formal and make a business plan for them and approach them in a structured manner to actually tell them the vision, mission, the planning, the strategy, the sales for 5-10 years, etc and so that is a real waiver and in my opinion, the biggest advantage.

Secondly, your friends trust you and hence convincing them is no big deal.

Thirdly, they are emotional about your business and success and hence with the intention of helping you, they will pour in the funds.

Lastly, they believe in you and know that you will not cheat them, concludes Rajat.

Wow! What financial management and apt strategy, isn't it? This is well supported by an example from USA, of an entrepreneur named Matthew Hogan, who endeavored to start his venture called *DataCoup* and yes, he did have his first round of funding from his friends.

When New York-based entrepreneur Matthew Hogan quit his steady job in finance to work on a startup idea, he told his two closest friends during a road trip to Atlantic City. A few months later, they each wrote Hogan a $25,000 check.

Many tech entrepreneurs take investment from friends and family to test the viability of an idea. They raise just enough to fund a developer's salary, office space, monthly rent, and a steady supply of ramen noodle soup.

It's a time-honored startup strategy, but it's a risky one. Hogan could make his friends rich, if his startup takes off. But if it craters, that lost $50,000, could haunt their friendship.

For Hogan, the investment buys him enough time to test the market opportunity for his startup, "DataCoup." If all goes according to plan, it will earn him a place at a competitive tech accelerator program like TechStars, which he can parlay into additional investment.

Above: Andrew Frank, Matthew Hogan and Brian Kauffman

"I'm solely investing in this idea because of Matt," said Andrew Frank, an investment banking managing director. "Anyone I didn't know with the same idea, I wouldn't have even looked at the slide deck," he admitted.

Hedge fund manager Brian Kauffman knows what he's getting himself into: he has made "six alternative investments" over the years. Five of them were in friends' startup companies. "If it [DataCoup] goes bad, I'd consider it to be a bad investment decision on my part," said Kauffman in a Skype interview. "I wouldn't blame Matt."

With friends like these, it's difficult to see a downside in taking their money. Typically, it's a darn sight easier than landing a seasoned angel investor.

Hogan's case aside, others advise caution in taking money from friends.

"I wouldn't take family and friends money if I had any other choice," said Angel List founder, Naval Ravikant in a recent interview. Unlike a professional angel investor like Mike Maples or Dave McClure, your wealthy Uncle Jim can't be called on for honest, critical feedback about your startup's business model.

Form the statement above, I am sure for every plus, there is a minus. For every god, there is a devil and for every advantage, there could be a disadvantage. So what were the shortcomings here as per Rajat?

"Yes every coin has two sides and so has this one also," says Rajat and further continues-

"The biggest drawback is that you cannot raise a big amount of fund and have to restrict with a smaller bit. Like I was looking for a bigger chunk of money but had to settle for limited fund.

The second drawback is that if you fail to provide the promised returns to your friend, you are at risk of losing your friendship with him and that is what scared me to the hilt because I did not want to lose my friends at any cost," says Rajat.

Well, those are some malevolence drawbacks but one needs to be a good planner in order to not have any such flips.

Happily unmarried started its operation only very recently and in a very short span of time has scaled height, thus making us surer of this funding process, because had it not been for this process, he would not have made it so far.

The Quirkiness in Happily Unmarried Products-

Wall Poster   **Rum Cushion Cover**   **Wall Posters**

Baywatch Hard Disk Cover   **Bean Bag Mobile Holder**   **Laptop Sleeve**

Happily unmarried, being a unique concept focusing on young India primarily caught the eye of his friends.

In funding, concept of the startup holds equal value. It's not that you get funded just for the sake of it by your friends but one also needs to be good at conceptualizing his startup in an appropriate way.

Simply put, it's like the Tom Cruise dialogue from the movie **'Jerry Maguire'** **"Show ME the MONEY!!!!"**

Also, it isn't that you aren't being professional if you tread this path, since you have been also generous enough to offer them the stake like Rajat did offering them 1% stake each.

Now that may sound a little diminutive a stake in a company but one must also know that the stake will be at par with the returns and the amount that has been put at stake.

Rajat had approx 3 lakhs from each of his 8 friends. He had the attributes of a good concept, a good promise that the proposal had made and so it made sense.

Happily Unmarried today is operating not only all over India but also in London, Paris and Dubai and its range of products is being appreciated all over with great consumer satisfaction that Rajat could achieve.

"Many of my friends have retained their stake with me still, since I have grown my business and it fortunately turned out to be a good bet for them to trust me and my concept, and invest their money with me," beams Rajat with a smile.

So dear readers, it is this innovative way of Rajat that has made him today what he is, had he not approached his friends, not asked them to trust him, most probably, his venture would have not picked up since we all know many of our ideas and startup die their death owing to lack of funds or must I say lack of proper innovative funding techniques which fit all.

Many of you may wonder, is this a one chance of luck that favored Rajat or can he repeat this process again, would he be interested in going the same way, if given a chance to raise funds??

'Of course, I would and there is no other method that I would adopt but stick to the same that I adopted to raise funds. There is no need to make any changes, but only a word of caution that I would like to give here and that is to make sure that you have made it clear to your friends that they don't expect the returns very soon and that it will take some time for the returns to start flowing in." Says Rajat.

Yes, that is a point well taken, it makes no sense to show a glorious picture to your friends about one's business prospects but to be safe and get them prepared to be patient enough.

Happily Unmarried proudly stands today at Delhi with a staff of 40, with the seed of innovative finding sown in by these 8 friends of Rajat.

This was a non-conventional source of funding and very innovative which helped Rajat to kick start his dream venture.

If I have to sum this story up as a final verdict, I would say, which Rajat also agrees with, this funding from large group of people helped Rajat catapult his position in front of the Venture Capitalist from whom very recently Happily Unmarried could manage a big source of funds. The VC liked the innovative and non-conventional way of raising funds and also well appreciated that the concept of Happily Unmarried was liked and trusted by so many of his friends. This further helped Rajat to have an upper hand as the VC appreciated it and this stood out to be a very strong point in favor of Happily Unmarried.

In the famous lines of George Soros, a Hungarian-American financier, businessman and notable philanthropist once said **"It is much easier to put existing resources to better use, than to develop resources where they do not exist."**

Bring them on and get going!

Fund-O- Drama

Funding Technique – **Funding through multiple friends**

Prerequisites: A clear business idea, set of trustworthy and close friends, passion and determination to make it happen

Time to fund	
	Less More
Ease of fund	
	Low High
Amount	
	Less More

11

Power2SME

Power2SME is India's first 'Buying Club' for SMEs (Small and Medium Enterprises) that started its operations in 2012 with the vision of 'empowering SMEs to enable India's growth story'. The company focuses on reducing the purchase prices for the SMEs through its innovative business model, thereby enhancing productivity and impacting the bottom line of SMEs in a positive manner.

It empowers SMEs to focus on their core business of driving growth and expansion, while the company takes on the role of sourcing input raw materials at the most competitive price points across multiple products in categories like Metals, Commodity & Engineering Polymers, Yarns, Paper, Chemicals, Rubber, Solar, etc. The company aggregates orders from SMEs and directly sources from suppliers of repute, thereby doing away with the middlemen.

Founder: Mr. R. Narayan

An entrepreneur for the last 19 years, with a strong corporate background, as Founder & CEO, Power2SME, Mr. R. Narayan's vision for the company's future is both bold and ambitious. Mr. Narayan started his career working in sales and marketing profile across Microsoft, Oracle and Tata. He has now set his sights on making Power2SME a billion dollar company in the next 5 years. This vision is based on the potential of the SME sector in India, which contributes over 40% of India's exports and 45% of India's industrial output, the current growth rate of Power2SME and Mr. Narayan's own proven entrepreneurial track record.

A Cost Accountant by education, sales and marketing professional by choice and an entrepreneur by spirit, Mr. R. Narayan set the overall direction for the business and overseas marketing, operational and business development efforts for Power2SME. With over 26 years of general management, sales & marketing experience, Mr. Narayan has worked closely with over 200,000 SMEs, across India, over the last 15 years, bringing a deep understanding of SMEs and their needs in an evolving economy. During his stint with Microsoft, Mr. Narayan managed the SME segment and distribution business of the company.

Before starting Power2SME, Mr. Narayan also set up Denave, India's largest technology powered sales enabling company with customers such as Nokia, Cisco, HP, Lenovo and Microsoft. Denave was a self-funded venture and he was responsible for scaling up the company from a team of 100 to a 3500 people organization over a decade and across APAC. He continues as a board member at Denave.

ABOUT POWER2SME

Power2SME breaks the traditional mould and has bought innovation to how raw materials are procured. The consensus being that procurement is the least exciting of domains, with the least amount of innovation possible. Add to this- procurement of raw materials and the general response would be that procurement has a defined traditional way of working with no scope of rehashing or rethinking. This was one industry that couldn't have been bitten by the technology bug. Mr. R Narayan, however, saw a big opportunity in this area and conceptualized Power2SME, aimed at totally redefining raw material procurement for the SMEs.

Power2SME, as the name suggests, is devised to empower the small and medium enterprises (SMEs) by functioning as a 'Buying Club' that helps them to benefit from economies of scale through collective buying from a large network of manufacturers. The company pools the demand of several SMEs, which enables it to obtain the best possible prices for the raw materials from a large pool of suppliers, thereby leading to significant cost savings.

Through an online portal as well as dedicated offline marketing, Power2SME helps SMEs in India to increase their profits by providing access to cheaper prices as well as financing for raw materials requirements.

GROWTH STORY

The company clocked approximately INR 1,206 CR (Several billions in USD) in the last financial year and has been clocking 3X growth in each year of its operation. Today, Power2SME boasts of more than 1, 00,000 registered SMEs users on it's platform and is eyeing the Unicorn status in the coming few years. So how did it actually come about?

"The idea to start Power2SME came about during my experience with the SME community on the field. I used to deal with both the SME and enterprise segments. I have seen price quotations that have been sent to an SME as well as a large enterprise, for the same product, where the variance was to the tune of 20-45%. This was mainly due to the size of the orders and SMEs' weak negotiation power. With 70% of Indian job market powered by SMEs, I felt this was an unfair gap between SMEs and enterprises. In 2009, I conducted research with the help of IIM-Lucknow students which validated this notion of unfair advantage enjoyed by corporates. At that point in time, I decided to build a portal where SMEs could submit their requirements and I would buy on their behalf."

THE DIGITAL ECOSYSTEM

He continues "Moreover, getting SMEs online wasn't much of a problem because of the e-commerce era that has emerged over the last few years. The widespread adoption of the internet gave a large number of individuals the option to search for options and order/procure items for their personal needs via internet". Implementation of GST further enabled expansion of Power2SME into non-operational markets with ease, thereby increasing the number of SMEs it can reach out to and increasing the number of transacting SMEs on its platforms by up to ten times in the next five years.

Power2SME is creating a digital ecosystem that enable SMEs to access raw materials and finance/credit on tap. Besides Power2SME.com, we have also created niche digital platforms for industrial buying and financial requirement - SMEShops.Com, FinanSME.Com

Back in 2012, Power2SME started off as India's first buying club for SMEs to source quality raw material but in our journey so far we realized the unattended demands of SMEs are not only restricted to raw materials but for other services as well. Power2SME today offers a digital SME ecosystem that addresses some key SME challenges with the firm's 'enterprise grade solutions' for SMEs. Its increased portfolio offering – addresses challenges in raw material procurement, Finance and MRO needs. Its B2B raw materials buying club (Power2SME.com) aggregates demand from SMEs for most commonly acquired raw materials (such as steel, polymers, yarns, chemical, etc.) and procures and sells these at competitive prices. Raw material accounts for 70 % of the recurring costs of manufacturing SMEs every month. Its platform (FinanSME.com) connects empaneled lenders with SMEs in order to provide working capital finance at better terms from banks and non-banking financial institutions for purchases on Power2SME. SMEShops.com is a one stop shop addressing SME MRO needs to meet the growing and frequent requirements of SME buyers for consumable industrial goods.

With our ecosystem we are trying and to some extent have been able to transform the way SMEs do their business, and they are able to:

- Strategize their procurement process, shorten their supply chain

- Plan their finances, keep a check on their credit limit and make better financial decisions

- Improve their profit margins

- Perform business activity on move – raise POs, place order from anywhere

- Overall, Power2SME is creating a healthy ecosystem for SMEs, Suppliers, Financial Institutes to work with each other seamlessly, which was not possible until sometime back

- Although, it is a win-win situation for all the stakeholders but for SMEs it is not only about addressing the challenges related to raw material or finance. With our ecosystem we are trying to transform the way SMEs do their business, and they are able to:

  ✓ Strategize their procurement process, shorten their supply chain

  ✓ Plan their finances, keep a check on their credit limit and make better financial decisions

  ✓ Improve their profit margins

  ✓ Perform business activity on move – raise POs, place order from anywhere

"I started Power2SME.com, with the sole objective of reducing the COGS (Cost of Goods Sold) for the SMEs, with seed capital of Rs. 20 Million USD. The inception of the company took place in January 2012 and it formally started operations in the month of June same year", adds Mr. Narayan.

Power2SME does not have a pre-defined product line. Basis our research, we knew that plastics, steel and polymers are the largest chunks of material that SMEs are looking for today. Hence, we decided to focus on these product categories in the first few months of our business. As of today, we focus on raw materials across categories, including steel, engineering & commodity polymers, chemicals and additives, yarns, solar, etc.

FUNDING

So how did the story of funding begin?

The company has raised over US $60 million funding from Inventus Capital Partners, Kalaari Capital, Accel Partners, Nandan Nilekani and the International Finance Corporation across five rounds of funding. In its Series A fundraising, Kalaari Capital had joined hands with Inventus Capital Partners to support our expansion plans in India. The company also raised funding from Accel Partners in the month of April 2013. The funding from Accel Partners was utilized by the company to further scale up operations, focus on new sectors while deepening its research into the SME sector and foray into new markets in India.

In the Series B funding, he raised USD 6 million from the three existing investors. This funding came about after a year of its operations. Further rounds of funding between 2014-2017 have witnessed Power2SME utilising the additional financing to continue geo expansion, accelerate product growth and innovation, invest in additional sales and marketing resources, and continue evaluating strategic acquisition opportunities. In 2018 alone, Power2SME expanded to 7 new markets. With an aim to offer an enabling operational environment to MSMEs, Power2SME expanded to 7 new markets in 2018 alone. Now operating in 16 offices across 23 states and Union Territories, Power2SME aims to ensure seamless functioning of enterprises in the country through its holistic business offerings

So, the natural question is should an entrepreneur look for investment from a single investor or look for multiple investors?

Says Mr. Narayan, "The collective intellect and strategic insights of multiple VC's enhances the probability of success for an entrepreneur. Since multiple investors are people from various backgrounds and expertise, it is really an added advantage as they bring in a complete newness and a varied approach to strategic thinking."

So since Mr. Narayan is so confident of this source of funding, would he want to ever repeat this again?

"Once you have gone through the initial round of fundraising successfully, it builds your reputation and carves out the path for the next rounds of funding. Once a company is able to engage with and excite the first couple of VCs, the path is simpler. I would not say that the first round of funding guarantees the next few rounds. As you grow as an organization, the growth of your business validates the success, stability as well as scalability of your business model, thereby setting it up for the future rounds of funding." Said Mr. Narayan.

So what would be Mr. Narayan's advice to those seeking this kind of funding? Would he recommend it to others?

"Yes, first and foremost, it is imperative to have a robust business plan that is based on facts instead of projections. The business plan should clearly outline the scalability of the business model as the concept gains acceptance in the marketplace. Also, complete transparency is recommended, when interacting with VC," says Mr. Narayan.

POWER2SME BUSINESS MODEL

I am curious to know what the Power2SME Business model is like.

Power2SME has an innovative business model which enables the small and medium enterprises to obtain the most optimal pricing for their procurement needs. The company pools the demand of multiple SMEs for raw materials for their business needs, thus allowing it to not only obtain the most optimal pricing, but also have an access to a larger pool of quality suppliers. Power2SME buys directly from the manufacturer and sells to SMEs, cutting out the middle link of distributors and wholesalers.

The services on offer go beyond being a match making platform as the firm takes complete ownership of the entire order process, including taking title of the goods, which ensure quality of the raw material at the best price with flexible payment options made available to SMEs. Power2SME also provides online platform that enables the SME customers to track all their purchases as well as undertake transactional activity such as placing new enquiries, checking price quotes, uploading purchase orders, checking status of delivery, account statement, notification of payment due etc.

Power2SME has SME clients with turnover ranging from 10 Million USD to 25 Billion USD and works with established suppliers such as SAIL, GAIL, Rathi Steel, Jindal Steel, Haldia Petrochemicals, amongst several others.

As part of the Power2SME's digital ecosystem, the company has launched two more platforms that ease operations for SMEs in two critical domains:

FINANSME

Access to finance has been identified as a key element for MSMEs to succeed, compete, create jobs and contribute to poverty alleviation in India. To strengthen the MSME framework, it was critical for Power2SME to devise a strategy focused on financial innovation that delivers capital to MSMEs and Growing Businesses in India- which will drive financial inclusion, a key to growth of entrepreneurship. Finance is the biggest problem for any SME as they struggle to meet their growth and operational requirements. Getting unsecured loans from banks is a lengthy process and requires lot of documentation. A CII report estimates that the total debt demand from SME is INR Rs. 33 trillion (Multi Billions in USD), out of which only 16% is being met by the existing banking system. There are various reasons why SMEs do not get enough financial support:

- Ticket size of loan & high transaction cost– The SME sector suffers from challenges of small ticket size of loan, low revenue per client, and incur high transaction cost due to which the traditional banking institutions refrain from financing these small ventures.

- Higher risk perception – Banks consider SMEs as a high risk sector owing to low or nil credit rating, higher rate of diversion of the funds, in many cases banks are unable to analyse creditworthiness of SMEs.

- Lack of collaterals - SMEs often fail to raise enough funds due to lack of collateral. Banks and other financing institutions prefer to give loans to entities with best collaterals and security such as residential property, thus crushing the efficiency and scope of growth of the small firms.

Power2SME acts a facilitator by bringing together SMEs & financial institutes on a common platform called **FinanSME**. The platform was launched in 2016 and 18 established financial institutes such as Axis Bank, Vistaar Finance, Religare and others have partnered with Power2SME for FinanSME.com. In order to ease the pressures on cash flow and facilitate smooth running of business, Power2SME helps provide bill finance facility to its partner SMEs. Their Bill Finance facility plugs in the mismatches in the cash flow and relieves the SMEs from worries on commitments.

SMESHOPS

Launched in 2016, **SMEShops** is the most user-friendly virtual marketplace to buy & sell goods online for SMEs in India and is one stop provider for all SME MRO (Maintenance, repair and operations) needs. With over 1.5 Lac SKUs already available on our website catalogue, SMEshops is one of the fastest moving in product acquisition and gaining seller trust from across geographies.

BRIDGING THE GAP

The Indian economy has the potential to become world's third-largest economy in the next decade, starting FY20. The 63 million units Indian MSME sector attributes to more than one-third of the total GDP of the country. In the near future, the contribution is only expected to increase while swiftly bridging the urban-rural intersection. Out of 63 million MSMEs about 19 million are involved in manufacturing products.

On a global platform India has the largest base of SMEs in the world after China. However, Indian SMEs contribute only 8-10 per cent to the nations GDP as compared to 60 per cent contribution by SMEs in China. This is a huge gap and major reasons holding back Indian MSMEs to contribute as much is lack of access to finance, fragmented market and supply chain, high price of raw materials as compared to their large counterparts, lack of digital adoption or modernization of their business.

Power2SME hopes to bridge this gap by bringing about a difference in quality, pricing (procurement of raw materials, credit interest rates), services (online market place to buy and sell & working capital requirements through our tie ups with FIs) to Manufacturing SMEs. They positively impact business efficiency, productivity, production cost and finally the profit margins.

SMEs	*Suppliers*	*Financial Institutes*
✓ Lower cost of raw material, hence improved margins ✓ Improved access to bank financing with cheaper ROI ✓ Transparency with GPS tracked deliveries ✓ Provide a level playing field to SMEs to list their products on B2B marketplace	✓ A fillip to institutional sales ✓ Reduced cost of client servicing ✓ Improved efficiency in working capital management	✓ Access to credit worthy SMEs who have passed robust ✓ Accreditation test at Power2SME ✓ Access to complete transaction history with P2S ✓ Negligible CAC

A snap shot of how it works:

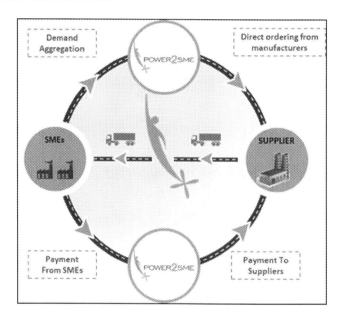

Power2SME's INITIATIVES FOR MSMEs

Spirit of Manufacturing Awards

While India is paving its way to become global manufacturing hub and cheering the great "Make in India" campaign. Embracing the same spirit, Power2SME along with TiE Delhi NCR has designed 'Spirit of Manufacturing Awards' that is fully aligned in the direction of recognizing the heroes of manufacturing sector

In the year 2013, Power2SME signed up with TiE Delhi; a global network of entrepreneurs, to roll out the **annual series** of 'Spirit of Manufacturing Awards'. This first-of-its kind of initiative was conceptualized and designed with the objective of applauding innovation and entrepreneurship in the manufacturing domain. The award aims to provide a platform to showcase some of the most promising start-ups in the manufacturing domain across the country. The awards provide the necessary visibility, ecosystem and mentorship for these start-ups to scale their operations in the sector.

SME Transformation Camps

Power2SME realizes the need of the hour is to not only to conceptualize and offer great technology platforms but also educate and familiarize SMEs to use such platforms. Hence, they designed the 'SME Transformation Camps' that work in close collaboration with SMEs across the country, via a series of events in different cities. The Camps focus on the areas of raw material procurement, technology and many other important aspects; with an aim to transform their businesses and provide them with competitive edge.

With several successful camps being attend by over 600+ SMEs in Pune, Noida, Kolkata, Faridabad and Rourkela, Cuttack, Delhi, Hyderabad, Bhubaneswar, Lucknow, Bengaluru, (All Major cities of India) we are now looking to ramp up the numbers **and hold over 20 camps in FY19.**

Parichay

Parichay is Power2SME's Business Referral Program. Through this program, existing clients can introduce their peers, business colleagues & friends in their network to buy Steel & Polymer raw materials through us. In return, they receive a reward.

SME Khabar

Power2SME keeps its existing and new clients abreast with latest news and industry trends through 'SMEKhabar.' It is a part of the online portal that disseminates daily news, articles, infographics and case studies.

An opt-in marketing tool that packages relevant and valuable developments or news on SME sector. It also provides entrepreneurial news & tips from across the globe. It is also comprised of original content in the form of articles, infographics, customer case studies & client testimonials. It has worked well for us – with 1, 00, 000 + subscribers for SME Khabar, Power2SME also receives feedbacks/requests from SME players on frequent basis.

Fund-O- Drama

Funding Technique – **Funding through multiple VC's**

Prerequisites: Own capital, robust business plan, transparent and passionate approach

Time to fund	Less More
Ease of fund	Low High
Amount	Less More

POWER TO THE PEOPLE

When they started off, Narayan wanted a holistic name which represents what they do. Inspired from the John Lennon song "Power to the people", the name Power2SME happened. "Even when hiring, we look for integrity, respect for individuals, and customer orientation. Employees spend more time in office than with their families; therefore, they should be looking forward to come to office. We have games and competitions as we believe in 'Play very hard,'" says Narayan, who is now heading a team of 358.

What is his advice to entrepreneurs? "Keep your eyes on what you do, not worry what world is doing."

12

VCare Financial

"Roughly 90-95% of the people do not have a financial planner. 90% of people do not know how compounding works, and how it can impact their future. People think they need to have a lot of money or they need to be from a wealthy family to have a financially rewarding future, which is not true. What makes people successful are the right habits they have and principles they follow that guides them to have a successful financial future. It's not about how much money one makes. A lot of people we don't know about have made fortunes by investing small amounts and are now on their way to achieving financial freedom."

Wow… that's something and this is how Milan opens our discussion.

VCare financial, a young startup run by two young guns, Milan and Milton D'Souza was founded as a platform for people to be able to break all myths and assumptions around investing and most importantly making your own money work for you. It was formed in late 2017.

The young founders based out of San Francisco Bay Area were born in Mangalore, India and were very passionate about investing and finances. This curiosity and passion led to the formulation of a business idea and here they are with VCare Financial.

So, what was their first exposure to this kind of a startup?

Milan says, "Exposure into these fields came because my father owned a restaurant when he was 19 and used to sell commodities. He would wisely make a lot of investment decisions and that got me curious about the whole idea of investments and business and money. I'm happy to say I have been passionately feeding the curiosity ever since."

Based in the heart and hub of the financial capital of California, the Silicon Valley and talking money is sure to capture eyeballs and today, VCare financial is quickly transforming itself as a leading Investment firm for people to beat their 401K challenges. The idea is simple; help people make money from their own money.

"We are a financial GPS, and we understand everyone has a different financial destination and goals. We customize our financial planning to fit their unique goals, like a GPS we guide them and show them how to get to their desired financial destination." Says Milan. He further adds, "We are into various product lines like Retirement Planning, Estate Planning, Tax Free Investment Strategies, Debt Management, Private Pension Plans, College Plans and more."

Milan and Milton are two brothers running the business successfully. Milan, the elder brother takes care of the Business Development and Marketing and Milton the younger one runs and executes things well. He is a Master at managing Business Operations.

So how did they go about launching this startup and how did they fund it?

Milan explains -As a business owner, we thought it was paramount to be extremely careful regarding how we finance our growth and at the same time be flexible about how we go about doing so. We didn't take any loans, or any outside funding. Luckily, I was fortunate enough to fund it through our personal funds, which I obtained by being in the real estate industry."

Incredible isn't it. For the uninitiated, you will be glad to know that the real estate business in San Francisco bay area is booming and is growing at a phenomenal rate with the bay area expanding exponentially in all directions. It's a real pleasure to see the growth here and the population too has grown multifold since the past few years making the real estate business very profitable.

That brings me to my next question of how did he manage to leave a booming industry like real estate and invest in his Financial venture?

"I was always clear of what I wanted. No doubt, real estate is doing very well, and I too had a good run when I was working in it, but my priorities were always clear of how and what I wanted. I am glad that the real estate industry funded my dream for me," says Milan candidly.

Milan and Milton, despite being in the booming real estate business and making good money decided to fund their dream venture - VCare Financial, slowly and steadily. They continued in the real estate industry until such time that they were confident that VCare Financial was stable.

So, how was it like funding your venture from an existing business and not opting for a loan since many believe that loans could be a better option rather than investing your own money?

To this Milan has a very interesting outlook and he says, "As an entrepreneur, it's our personal belief that we get paid to take risks that have an asymmetric risk to reward ratio. We must take risks that don't require too much capital outlay and try investing for growth in your business in an organic way. By committing little capital to new business ideas for growth, we become flexible to try new things and ensure that too much of our capital is not tied up to one idea that could diminish our return on invested capital. This also facilitates us with things that work."

So, what do they believe was the good or not so good about this kind of funding?

Milan and Milton have many outlooks on this form of funding, but one thing that stands out for them is –

"One of the advantages of not taking a loan and not aggressively investing for the sake of growth is that it can put less pressure on the entrepreneur, which might lead them to do stuff that might not be good for the long run. On a psychological level however, we believe that entrepreneurs should also invest their personal funds in the business."

Well that's a conspicuous statement.

He further explains the same through an analogy. "It's like when people cook, and they know that they have to relish their own cooking, they may be more careful and guarded about it and in the same way by being careful about investing we can create growth that is intrinsic, foundational and sustainable."

Therefore, to put things in perspective as an Author, I believe that the passion calling that was there within them always ensured that the focus is not shifted. Despite being in a booming industry they never lost the grit and determination to start their own venture in another equally flourishing industry.

Most of the time we withdraw from a business idea because we assume that it will be difficult to arrange funds for executing the same. We often lose our passion and will in the name of survival and paying our bills. But if you are keen and aware of how you like to do things, you will be able to deliver more.

The three good things to take away from their story is -

1- They never lost focus on what they wanted and were keen to always have that going. Because of that at a very young age, they could achieve their dream without taking a single dollar loan from their father or from any bank/financial institution.

2- Became a part of an industry which was not in their area of interest but worked sincerely in it to have their bills paid and also arrange for investment for their dream venture; the now robust startup, VCare Financial.

3- These brothers worked as a team, shared the same vision and mission. Never said 'Never'. They worked in tandem with each other and ensured success.

Milan and Milton for sure know where they are going and what the future should look like for their company. This belief prompts me to ask them of any financial insight that they think would be relevant here and also justifies their funding methodology. To this Milan says -

"When business is based on investing on tangible assets for growth, and if intangible assets don't become the primary driver for earnings or growth within the business, the former can diminish the return on investing capital of the business over short or long period of time. To combat the fate of investing in tangible assets which is the case for most businesses, it is of the utmost importance to build Goodwill.

"This certainly helps in the long run and keeps return on investing capital stable. Goodwill could mean good customer service, pleasant experience for customer, ultimately putting customer's current or changing priorities among other things on the frontline for business growth. By doing that you will perhaps have repeated and loyal customers, which in turn can reduce your marketing costs."

That's a real good word of advice from them which helps the investors differentiate between the importance of investing in tangible and intangible assets and bringing out the importance of creating goodwill.

So now that we know that they are good and have had a good run with this kind of funding, would they recommend this type of funding to others?

Milan says, "Depends on their circumstances, in our case we needed small capital to start the business. Even if we start a business that has larger fixed costs, we would initially use our money then perhaps start the second round of funding if needed."

Well that makes complete sense, VCare Financials.

Startups! Finding Funding

Fund-O- Drama

Funding Technique – **Funding from your Real Estate Business.**

Prerequisites: Sincere efforts in business used for funding and clear focus and vision. Sequential planning and tracking the same in regular intervals.

Time to fund	⬜⬜
	Less More
Ease of fund	⬜
	Low High
Amount	⬜⬜⬜
	Less More

13

Makkhan Maar Ke
(With a Dash of Butter)

 Makkhan Maar ke, from the house of Makharia Hospitality (P) Ltd is a food delivery Chain situated in Aundh, Pune, India. Spread across an area of 1250 sq.ft, the delivery center tingles the taste buds of every food connoisseur with its North Indian fare. Conceptualized by restaurateur Mr. Piyush Makharia, it offers the finest dining experience with authentic & true to the roots North Indian cuisine stirred up by chefs who tread all the way from Garwhal. The menu spoils you for choice with a rich array of starters, main course and desserts for both vegetarians and non-vegetarians. Weight watchers need not be disappointed, Makkhan Maar ke has a rich selection of healthy kebabs too.

Founder: Piyush Makharia

 Piyush Makharia, the adoring and passionate founder of this North Indian cuisine specialty chain, is a production engineer by qualification from Sinhagad Institute of Technology, Pune, India. Piyush was not the one to sweat it out on a production plant. Since childhood, he has been very fond of what he eats and has been an ardent food critic at home always.

His playful criticism led him to realize his dream job and today he is doing what he likes the most.

Makkhan Maar Ke! (With a Dash of Butter) Interesting name! Waters your mouth, right?? And yes your guess is as good as mine. It is a chain placed cozily in Aundh vicinity of Pune. As appealing is the food of this Punjabi themed Chain, equally interesting is its tale of funding. It was funded by the 40 year old run family business of Car Hiring. Family business funding is not something of jeopardy as it may seem. Moreover, don't we all at least once depend on our family to get financed? There is also this interesting thing about family funding, and that could be a nice family drama enfolded behind it, which in this case was not much, owing to pure understanding and strong ambitions of Piyush and his family.

As mentioned in his intro, Piyush Makharia, a production engineer from Sinhagad Institute, always had wild dreams. Friends find him charming and a maverick to that extent that has love for music, friends and his food. He has that vivacious energy, which goes all out, and the contrasting combo of an emotional and affectionate gentleman.

So digging further, did he always want to be an engineer?

"I never wanted to do engineering although my approach in life is very technical and analytical and like typical Indian families, I too was the victim of my family's expectations from me. They wanted me to wear the hat of an engineer because of which I had to do engineering," says Piyush.

So how did this Production engineer transit to a food delivery chain owner?

"I was always keen to do something different and then suddenly I started developing the passion of cooking. I always loved food and had a good knowledge of some good cuisines, courtesy, passion and my innumerable travels around the globe. Since I was a passionate foodie, I had apt knowledge, so I thought to myself, why not? And therefore the idea of restaurant struck me," says Piyush.

This was it and so the idea of Makkhan Maar ke was born! But what did Piyush think about the funds? How did he go about it?

"I had 2 options. Either strike a deal with some bank or a financial institution and get going or ask my family. I decided for the latter. I asked them to loan me some money to begin rolling. I guess a known devil is better than an unknown devil," laughs Piyush.

Family business funding! Sounds very normal! So what could be fascinating about this?

Don't we have this system day in and out where we get paid for by our family?

They are there from the time we are growing up till we don't settle down in life, get married and land a good job; don't our families support us always? Sometimes we get the support even after that. So what's so new in this?

The answer you may certainly come out with is that there is nothing new, but how many of us have actually rationalized or may be scrutinized this source of funding? What goes into it and what could be the outcome? So let's precipitate and find out about the same.

To understand, let us first learn that Piyush is not the only one here and there are a lot of people in this space. Budding entrepreneurs often turn to a lender that overlooks weak points, provides flexible terms, and offers a dream-come-true interest rate: which is the Bank of Mom or Dad. Without an established track record, start-ups often have trouble getting a traditional bank loan or funding from venture or angel investors. So, after tapping their savings, founders often turn to informal investors, which usually means family members, as in the case of Piyush.

For finances from outside, many people will opt for a loosely structured deal in which, for example, repayment may start only when a company has reasonable cash flow and can afford to make payments — a position many businesses don't reach until three to five years down the road, if at all. Such an arrangement doesn't raise expectations of prompt repayment. But such vagueness can lead to problems and confusion later on, prompting some experts to urge putting into writing whether funds are a loan, gift or an investment. Still, terms of the agreement need close attention. Failure to collect interest or a repayment might prompt the Internal Revenue Service to decide if the "loan" was actually a gift and impose gift tax and other penalties.

Such arrangements combine best wishes, a pay-me-when-you-can attitude, and few expectations of a meaningful return. That might be the most realistic view of family financing. So in many cases, it might be wise to not formalize the loan since doing so can raise expectations that it will be repaid in full.

Coming back to Piyush, how did he make this happen?

"My family has been in Car Hirers business from the last 35 years. In Pune, we have a fleet of 45 cars of various models and types. We have customers from various industries and cater to them as per their customized requirements. But this did not excite me and hence I urged upon my family to part with some funds from their business for me to start my own restaurant," says Piyush.

Piyush further continuous "Like I said, I did not want to have a bank deal and so I asked my family to punch in the money. I had some of my savings, which were invested, but they were not sufficient to provide the needed capital for a startup and so I turned towards my family for further financial support. I had options of getting funds from friends but I thought why not family business funds? Since I was a beginner and wanted loan from my family, they ensured that I realize the importance of funds being let out to me and hence made the ride a little tough for me"

Piyush's family did lend him the money but also ensured that he did have the same on merit.

Although it is your family's business funds, yet the drill here is not a cake walk. Piyush has two brothers, an elder and a younger.

"Yes, at that time, my elder brother who worked with KPMG was based out of South Africa and my younger brother is into our family business of Car rentals. He is managing the show," says Piyush.

So how the drill was finally managed? Didn't he have any reservations from his younger brother since he was at the helm of managing his family business?

"My family fortunately is very broad minded. My younger brother was also very supportive and so was my elder brother. Since they were keen that I follow my passion, they really did not have any brunt against my plans. Having said that the fact remains that there obviously was some concern of having their balance sheet deprived of a good 3.5 million USD of solid cash for my chain. But then I was determined to seek funds from them and I did not want to fall in the trap of loans, interest and principal repayment in my very first venture and hence I thought of trying this source," says Piyush.

So what was Piyush's experience of using these funds?

"It may seem like a cool way to raise funds from your family, but it isn't. You need to really convince them hard that you have the capability to manage the venture you need to invest in and that you will justify. I too did the same. Not that my family business is very cash rich but here, the stakes were high and therefore to get the funds out of their kitty was not a piece of cake. My father being that traditional businessman was more concerned about the maths of my business and my mother was more concerned about the quality and service of the food that I would offer. For them, this also meant that the current family business would get impacted if I falter and the Murphy's Law kept striking me every now and then. There has to be no wrong to believe in it and hence I kept my spirits high and was quite confident about it," completes Piyush.

Did his passion therefore become a platform for family drama?

Piyush heartily laughs and says "Yes, kind of, but more than drama, it was the concern than anything else, they were concerned about me."

If we spend some time and look at this source in a holistic way, then I remember an article by Stephen J. Simurda which said that even Shakespeare makes a point in Hamlet that has become something of a conventional wisdom these days. Many people feel that it can only lead to trouble to loan money to those close to you. At the same time, family members loan each other money all the time, for reasons ranging from the serious (starting a new business or buying a first home) to the spurious (paying off the $300 you just lost betting on football game). What are these lenders risking, besides just mony, when making these loans?

Loans to family members can be expressions of trust and care, but they can also lead to distrust and alienation. Parents who loan money to children have been known to try unfairly to influence the recipient's personal decisions, such as where to live or what career to pursue. On the other hand, borrowers who haven't thought clearly about the implications of their loan can get defensive when asked about repayment.

But all is not gloomy in the hood and there certainly is a brighter side to it as well. Like Author Bonnie Conrad mentions, the two biggest pros about this kind of funding are -

One of the biggest advantages of borrowing money from family is that you are likely to pay a lower interest rate than you could get at a bank or credit union. Many lenders are reluctant to lend money to startup companies without a proven track record, and even when they are willing to lend, the interest rates they charge can be very high. By borrowing the funds from family members, you can avoid these big interest rates and have more money to run your business.

Of course it is important for all business loans, even those financed by family members, to be properly structured. The startup money you receive should be structured as a loan, with a written loan agreement, monthly payment terms and interest rates clearly spelled out. This will help you avoid disputes in the future and protect your interests in the event there are problems down the road.

Secondly, family members may be willing to negotiate favorable repayment terms for your new business loans, while traditional lenders will generally be less flexible. For instance, you might be able to write a loan in which the repayment does not begin for six months to a year down the road. This gives you time to get your new venture off the ground without worrying about servicing the debt right away. While your brother-in-law or grandmother is likely to agree to this arrangement, a traditional bank might be less understanding. No matter what terms you work out, it is important to put them in writing. All parties must understand and agree to the terms of the loan and the repayment arrangement before signing the loan paperwork.

So does Piyush believe it is a fruitful way of raising funds-?

"Yes, everything has two sides like a coin, and so it has its pros and cons too. Let's get straight to know them-

Pros- Loans from family can be obtained quickly since they share with the entrepreneur a relationship that is based on a more personal level. Business owners have the benefit of not paying back interest or providing a monthly payment as bank loans require.

One can ease out and have more margins on his deliverables, since there is no clause of repayment on capital.

Offers the family for probable growth of its business empire provided one succeeds in it.

And in my opinion, the cons would be-

The fact that one may give up more ownership of their company. More the partners involved, more the profits will be divided amongst all. Through Family business finding, the family members may feel that they have the right to offer suggestions concerning the management of the business. Their suggestions may sometimes be contrary to the entrepreneur's strategy and may even strain personal relationships. Entrepreneurs should repay the loans as quickly as possible in order to avoid interpersonal conflicts among family members.

Unfortunately, if you make loss, the balance sheet of your existing family business suffers a huge setback.

Lastly, there could be unfortunate disputes with your family members and sour relations at times of adversity." Says Piyush.

Fortunately for Piyush, Makkhan Maar ke is 13 years old today, having been established in 2005 and serving delicacies from the north Indian stable has helped create a good name for itself in Baner, Aundh and other high-profile locales of Pune. With a staff of 5 people, Makkhan Maar Ke now proposes to shift out of its current facility to a sprawling 3000 Sq. ft place with lounge and bar as its additional amenities on offer in Baner close to his current location.

"This could have been possible only because of that one risk I took of involving funds of my family." Says Piyush.

So would Piyush want to repeat this source?

'Yes, I would love to but will advise some caution, which I did not consider in my case. I would suggest before opting for this source, one must have his pencil calculations in place like the capital cost of furniture, place, etc sorted out, the kind of working capital he may want, etc and the kind of business you expect to generate and your probable target market, as this gives a broader overview to the family of your plans and also indirectly induces confidence in them since you have your homework in place," says Piyush.

Makkhan Maar Ke today proudly stands tall with a lineage of some very loyal customers who would regularly want to relish the exotic dishes doled out by Makkhan Maar ke.

He has had senior corporate executives, TV stars and Producers amongst other food lovers and Piyush has surely had an impeccable rendezvous with them to cherish forever.

Fund-O- Drama

Funding Technique – Family Business funding

Prerequisites - Established family business, work out modalities of your startup to put up as a thought to your family, strong family bond.

Time to fund	
	Less More
Ease of fund	
	Low High
Amount	
	Less More

14

Simplibuy

Simplibuy Simplibuy™ Technologies, incorporated in 2010 in Pune, is a privately held technology company involved in creation of a hyper local shopping discovery information system. Simplibuy is ranked amongst National Top 50 emerging companies by NASSCOM in 2013 and is also Red Herring Asia 100 finalist this year. Angel funded by Ecosystem Ventures (California), Everest Wealth Management (Switzerland) and other angels from Singapore and India. it's a great showcase of great collaboration amongst investors to build a truly global organization.

Founder: Arun Purohit

 Arun Purohit, a former Air Force officer and a BITS PILANI is the hustler. He drives the product strategy and marketing initiatives. A certified project manager, he focuses on operational efficiencies. Wicfy, their product was conceived as a conversation between him and his best friend during a train journey. Helping users find and locate the cheapest sellers in

town opens a wonderful world of opportunities and challenges. He is obsessed about solving this problem for a large variety of products. An avid squash, guitar and chess player, he spends free digital time hanging out on twitter and Quora. He is also a big fan of vegetarian street food.

Convertible debt is a popular method in the States to raise initial funds when the valuations are difficult to decide. Dave Guttman and Orlando Saez of City Scan (cityscan.com) raised $1.2 Million through convertible debt. In 2011, SV Angel and Yuri Milner offered a convertible debt of $150,000 to every pass out from

YCombinator. Save one, the rest took it. However, India is a different story where it is almost impossible to get funded using this approach. However, we found an exception in Arun, who convinced not one or two, but a dozen investors to put in 40 Lakhs in his patented Price Comparison Platform – Simplibuy.

Arun Purohit, Founder, Simplibuy.in has successfully raised 4 Million USD from twelve people as convertible debt. He says "It was a jarring journey, since to convince people here in India for the convertible debt is a herculean task."

Convertible debt is a complex tool and for people who do not want to Google it, – here is a quick primer.

Convertible debt is an investment that "converts" into equity in the future usually at a discount to your next funding round price and sometimes has a "cap" (maximum price).

Let's get into an example – The Garage Angels Club invests USD 5 Million in Mammoth Inc, a startup, as a convertible debt. The terms of the debt are a 20% discount and automatic conversion after a qualified financing of USD 10 million. After a year, Mammoth Inc. signs a term sheet with Big Ventures for investing 50 million USD in them and value the company at 100 Million USD. At that point, Garage Angels debt will automatically convert to equity at a valuation of USD 80 Million (20% less than USD 100 million whiz kid). So, Garage Angels will get shares worth USD 5 million at a valuation of 800 million USD or 16% of Mammoth Inc. In simple terms, the value of the company is determined at a later date and initial investors are offered some discount to cover the gap between the initial investment and the later date.

Arun adds, "convertible debt is valuable for initial funding as the valuation of a startup is hard to determine, especially if the startup is pre-revenue and only in the idea phase. How do you put a value on the potential of the team or idea? It is easier for a startup to put off that question until they have some traction and social proof. Convertible debts are attractive for a startup because it delays this issue. While adding a cap essentially prices the round, it does leave a range of options, so it is more attractive to the startup. However, it does leave the investor in an ambiguous state because he can never be sure how much equity he will get for his investment. Indians, because they do not like ambiguity, prefer to avoid this route as much as possible."

Taking Arun's case as a clue, I have noticed and as per a recent article published by Jayadevan, which says that while equity financing remain the primary way of raising early stage capital in India, convertible instruments are showing some early signs of picking up. A small number of startups, like price comparison site Find Yogi or mobile publishing platform Mobstac, have raised early funding using c- notes. Indusdiva, Gazemetrix, Instamojo, Chargebee and a few others have also used convertible instruments to raise funds.

For startups, the obvious advantage is that it won't have to value the company early on and dilute too much equity. It is also less distracting, consumes less resources and time. For investors, it's a quick way to enter a hot startup. But is it the right way to do it? What are the do's and don'ts?

"We weren't sure of the valuation when we wanted money. So the idea was to raise convertible equity with a discount to the investor whenever we raised the next round. That way, things moved very fast for us," Naman Sarawagi, the founder of FindYogi told NextBigWhat.

There's been a lot of debate around it, especially in the Silicon Valley where convertible instruments are widely used. The general consensus is that it is startup friendly. And depending on how you look at it, not very investor friendly.

"As long as the demand-supply gap exists in India, convertible debts won't take off," says Mukund,

Mohan, Director at Microsoft Ventures. Microsoft which recently realigned its startup activities under the Microsoft Ventures umbrella, invests in the form of convertible debts.

For startups, convertible debt is a good thing though. It takes off the pressure to value a company early on. "That largely supports the "angel investors" and founders are generally keen to work together, more often than not, some angel investors are keen to lend not just money but also their expertise to the startup. In this scenario, getting into valuation discussions can be quite adversarial," says Kunal Walia, the Managing Partner at Khetal Advisors, a boutique investment bank.

These scenarios can be apt as far as startups are concerned, as in the founders, but what about the investors? What is it for them? Is this really a good platform for them to invest in? As in the case of Arun, why did a dozen investors agree to fund Arun with a convertible debt?

"Great concepts have great stories and so my story too had that great concept. When I pitched my business idea to my friend, he immediately agreed to pump in 270,000 USD but that was not to be enough and hence, he blasted my concept to all his allies in his network and bingo, we hit the target. People were happy and feeling great about the concept and that is how we managed to pull their attention. Now the next thing for us was to convert their attention into this debt and hence I offered them an interest rate at 10% per year on their funds and promised them discounted equity share certificates once the valuation of my company is done".

For investors, the preference for debt vs equity is less clear. Sometimes investors are so eager to get the opportunity to invest in a company that they will put their money into a convertible note and let the next round of investors set the price. They believe that if they insisted on setting a price now, the company would simply not take their money. Sometimes investors believe that the compensation, in the form of a warrant or a discount, is sufficiently valuable that it offsets the value of taking debt vs equity. Finally, debt is senior to equity in liquidation so there is some additional security in taking a debt position in company vs an equity position. For early stage startups, however, this is not particularly valuable. If a startup fails, there is often little or no liquidation value.

He further continues, "In spite of no rationale behind us for the funds we needed, we were confident that we did hit it with the investors based on our idea and the same happened and we were fortunate enough to get the desired kick off funds of USD 4 Million."

Therefore the investors found a dual treat to them, one, the interest rate @ 10% and secondly, the equity conversion at discounted rate. A kind of double whammy!

Arun realizes that he was extremely lucky and thinks that there could be some glitches that one must be careful of. Therefore he warns other startups of the following -

"Indian investors have a mental block to fund technology platforms and to convince them for it is a huge task. Add the fact that you are suggesting a convertible debt and you are looking at a long battle. It took me a number of rounds with the people before they got convinced. However it did become easier after the first few guys who I had to struggle a lot with."

"Second, since the amounts are small, the capital raised also will definitely be small and hence hiring manpower is not fulfilled and you are the only one doing the bout of things. I had to run around everywhere, convincing investors, getting the paperwork done and also running my business."

"Lastly, owing to limited funds, the expectation management of Investors becomes a challenge as one needs to be really skillful in managing funds and the operations as well in sync. I had to promise the investors a weekly update report so that they would know exactly what is going on."

But before you write off this technique, Arun shows us light at the end of the tunnel. He feels that you can pull it off if you take care of some basic things.

"Making the venture sound exciting and seeing the world changing gives Investors a high of investing and being part of the Next Big Thing after Google and Apple."

"Ask small amounts from a large number of people than a large amount from one angel. With smaller amount, people have fewer questions."

"Get a couple of anchors who are willing to bat for you. Indians are comfortable investing when they see others have already taken the plunge. In my case my friend helped me right through to convince the other investors."

"Work with the investors to show them how Convertible Debt takes less paperwork and is overall less expensive to execute. While normal Angel Funding can take months, Convertible debt can be executed in days."

He also points out a big advantage when you raise convertible debt from a large group of investors. "The founders retain the majority of the voting stock in the company. That means when it comes to making a decision that requires a vote, you will be in a better position to execute your plan. You might get a board seat request with a larger debt investment, but typically in a seed stage offering, you won't have to worry about that."

Troy Henikoff, CEO of Chicago based accelerator, Excelerate Lab says "Three years ago, I don't think I'd even heard of convertible debt, whereas several startups from this year's class are turning to such financing."

Yes, that's true; a host of startups are making this model popular owing to several advantages attached to it. Be it the Indian or the American startup scenario, the feeling is mutual.

Would Arun want to repeat this source?

'Of course, but I will make a change, which I could not comprehend earlier and that is to get my expense analysis done and equity ratio decided with the help of a senior financial advisor. This will allow me to be surer of my rationale as an entrepreneur and can accordingly facilitate my moves better." Says Arun.

Arun's design of funding has helped him garner the second round of funding from a billionaire entrepreneur and angel, this time a very big undisclosed amount and not from India but USA. His angel was impressed by his idea and the whole approach to getting his first round of funds. Simplibuy, a technology based platform brings together host of interesting sites of fungible mass products for its users to know the best deals available in market today. In other words, Simplibuy brings the world to you so as to enable you to buy faster and better.

"We will invest the funds on user acquisition, expanding the team, and replicating our model in multiple cities in the country. Since the platform is based on user-generated content, we will have to focus on user engagement and discoverability of the platform. Marketing will be a key focus area for us and we will do online marketing, as well as release informative product videos (about the platform) on video hosting sites like YouTube, Vimeo, etc." said Arun.

In Arun's final words before bidding us adieu *"You will know what to buy, when to buy and also where to buy when you get acquainted to Simplibuy."*

Fund-O- Drama

Funding Technique – Convertible debt from a host of small investors.

Prerequisites: High adrenaline and mind blowing business idea. a couple of anchor investors and willingness to do the rounds.

Time to fund	Less More
Ease of fund	Low High
Amount	Less More

15

Mobikon Technologies

 Mobikon Technologies was founded as a Mobile Platform in 2008. It quickly transformed itself as a mobile platform for hotels and then became a Customer Engagement & data Platform for Hospitality in 2011.

In 2012, it was funded by Jungle Ventures and shifted to Singapore. Mobikon today works with over 4000+ restaurants, engaging over 40 Million Diners and powering over 4 Million instore Feedbacks.

Founder: Samir Khadepaun

 Samir Khadepaun, after studying from PICT (Pune, India), went on to study at the prestigious Monash University. After dabbling with various jobs, he decided to become an entrepreneur in 2009. Seeing mobiles taking over the world, he decided to create a mobile technology company, which was converted into a Customer Engagement Platform. He now lives and works in Singapore.

An Engineering student passes out from one of the most prestigious colleges of Pune in Computer Engineering in 1999. Ten years later, he travels to USA on a credit card to visit thirty of his alumni mates in USA. He traverses the whole of USA, meeting the alumni network. In the mornings, he pitches his idea to his mates and crashes in with the same people at night. After one month, he takes back a plane to India, with cheques worth USD 10 million in his pocket. This is the seed money for Samir Khadepaun's debut venture – Mobikon.

"I had a great idea of building a mobile platform for customer engagement but no money. After asking my family and friends, I realized that it would just not be enough. It was then that I figured out that lot of my US alumni had earned tons of money and maybe would be interested in investing in my idea. Good for me, I had been in touch through mails with almost forty of my alumni. That's what gave me the idea of building a business plan, creating some financial projections and jumping onto the next plane to US. Mobikon," he laughs, "was born in US, not in India."

He further continues "Once I reached USA, I was on a kind of road show wherein I was visiting each of my mates at their location and explaining the proposal to each one of them. It took me a good one month to do so and try and explain to them my idea and how I am going to go about the same. Some of them were convinced about the idea, some were not and finally my hard work paid off with seven out of them agreeing to fund me. I could finally manage to raise nearly 10 million USD says Samir.

So why would the Alumni network fund you? -

"A known devil is better than an unknown devil. You have spent a good four years with them, you have laughed with them, cried with them, made all kinds of dialogues, be it for your emotions, your crushes or your family. In four years, you have built a trust, which remains forever. Look at how all the IIT alumni in US who keeps giving tons of dollars back to their alma mater. Vinod Gupta of InfoGroup gave $2Mn to IIT Kharagpur. Phaneesh Murthy and Kris Gopal have contributed crores to IIT Chennai. The alumnus in US always wants to retain ties with their college and their country. And a small investment in India somehow makes them feel more connected to their roots".

The idea should be a global play. Most Indians based out of US do not believe local Indians.

USA has always been a happy hunting ground for startups from India. Technology startups have especially found it much easier to raise funds from the States.

Valuations in US for technology companies are always higher than in India. I asked a couple of investors and they feel that the difference could be as high as two to three times.

US investors are also more amenable to fund companies at a concept level. Indian investors prefer to invest in revenue generating companies and at a much later stage.

Hah. This is critical. And therefore, this technique will only work with US Alumni as Indian mates may not feel the same gap. The other interesting thing, which ties this idea solely to US, is more financial. In US, it is difficult to get good returns on small amounts of money like $10-20 thousands. Savings and FD (Fixed Deposits) rates are negligible; investing in share markets is complex and not very lucrative, and property investments need more money. Many of the Indians who have shifted to US have collected small fortunes and are looking for a way to invest with bigger returns. Investing in Indian startups is an interesting option. And investing in an alumnus gives you the safety. Plus, old mates are not usually greedy and are willing to take a small amount of equity for their investments. Try it with Indian friends and you will have to shell out much more."

"Being in touch with your alumni is critical. I was in touch with around thirty of my alumni through mails and phone."

"Having a good idea with a good business plan is another. US people have seen lot of entrepreneurship activities and so they have a nose for a viable idea. The idea needs to be exciting and world changing for them to catch on. After I shared my idea with them, they showed a preliminary interest. Those egged me on to bite the bullet and swipe my credit card for the USD 10 million to US."

The idea is very critical in this mode of funding. Remember most of technology guys stay in and around Silicon Valley. So, they have all been part of the birth of the likes of Twitter and Facebook. So even if they cannot become entrepreneurs themselves, their whole approach is big. They are only interested in companies which will become a billion dollars. So, make sure your idea has the required glam when you pitch it.

"The other thing which I feel impressed them was my zeal and passion. I mean it was evident that I am very enthusiastic about this deal as I came on credit to USA, stayed like a meager in their house and therefore you need to have both an idea and a passion to make it big."

So now that it is almost four years since this escapade and the rolling out of his venture, what is his take? -

"Firstly, since they know you, the trust is immense. Unlike investors, they do no act like watchdogs who would be continuously bothering you for their returns. The other benefit is to have their knowledge and wisdom at no cost. Some of them are geeks and have helped me immensely in my technical platform. Yes, good mentors at no cost have been a big bonus."

This approach comes with truckloads of secondary benefits. The biggest advantage is obviously access to great technology resources, which are not only limited in India but are also very costly. Also top up funds become accessible. If you are doing well, then the alumni network is happy to put in more funds. Even Samir, when later required more funds, was able to pick some more funds from the same people. This is not true for India. Usually individual investors in India will not put funds in the same company and prefer to diversify. The US guys also look great on the advisory panel. Many of them work for the likes of Google and Amazon and make for great celebrity value.

Any more thoughts from Samir on how to approach the network?

"Yes, it is a perfect way," emphasizes Samir and continues, "and I honestly see no flip to this sourcing apart from some advice that I would like to give here. Firstly, don't over commit, if you cannot deliver, don't commit. Secondly, whatever commitment you have made, don't under perform. Also, if you perform to your best, you are bound to succeed and lastly, steer away from those who have very high expectations from you in terms of returns or deliveries as they will cause you more harm than good."

Funding from the US Alumni Network:

Pros:
Funds can be raised quickly
Not as much trouble as Angel Investors from India
Benefits in kind – Tech know how, Advisory Board, good references Top up funds if required

Cons:
Idea must be original, technology based and global Huge effort in convincing the alumni
High risk of reputation loss in case commitments not met
You should have a good background. Past deeds can haunt you forever.

Will he do it again?

"I am already doing it for another start up, but with a change. This time I am trying to have like-minded and intellectual people also on board who can contribute through their knowledge, experience and deliveries, which is also a very essential element".

Samir did not let his alumni down. After four years of a bumpy ride, he is now growing at a fast clip with Mobikon, servicing over four thousand restaurants. During the journey, he has already provided exit to a few of his mates at higher valuations. In 2012, Singapore Govt and Jungle Ventures funded him with two million dollars. And eventually company raised $12 Million from couple of more VC's and planning to build a global company.

"Thanks to my alumni, I am now the largest player in my area in the whole of Asia. In three years, I will make it the world."

Fund-O- Drama

Funding Technique – College Alumni based out of USA. (India is a different story)

Prerequisites: Good relationship with your alumni network, high adrenaline and an earth shattering (well, at least a grand) idea.

Time to fund	
	▢ Less More
Ease of fund	
	▢▢ Low High
Amount	
	▢▢ Less More

16

IAchievegroup.com

In pursuit of their mission, the Achieve group has developed a business model that empowers people to unleash their potential and become successful entrepreneurs. An intelligent collaboration of knowledge and experience, they specialize in leveraging the power of social media to help individuals establish their own global online businesses.

Founder: Tarun Gupta

Tar un Gupta i s an Indian- American entrepreneur with over 20 years of experience in Information technology, Business Development and Public Speaking. He provides coaching and mentorship in the areas of business ethics, leadership, time management and wealth management to entrepreneurs across the globe. Tarun completed his BE in computer engineering from Pune University and Master of Business Administration in Finance and Marketing from the prestigious Kellogg School of Management.

Tarun has been the knight in the shining armor when it comes to funding as he opted for not a VC (Venture Capital), not an Angel investor or a bank loan but the honorary of investing his own personal savings.

More entrepreneurs are willing to put their own money on the line for business, according to the second annual Kauffman Foundation / Legal Zoom survey of new business owners.

While fewer entrepreneurs experienced difficulties gaining access to credit in 2013, the survey findings show that more decided to invest their own personal savings into their new ventures, jumping 20% to 86% overall in 2013. Additionally, more new entrepreneurs turned to credit cards, retirement savings and bank or home equity loans than they did in 2012.

Legal Zoom CEO, John Suh says this is a good sign for the outlook on Main Street. "Few actions correlate more directly with economic confidence than personal

investment. Investing personal savings to start a business when credit is readily available signals high conviction in the future," said Suh in a statement released by LegalZoom.

So coming back to Tarun, what was his story and how did it turn around for him?

The turnaround of funding-

Tarun migrated to USA in 1993 with nothing in his pocket, albeit with eyes full of dreams and passion to make it big on his own.

"I graduated from Pune and went on to do my MBA from Kellogg's Institute, USA. I did my MBA in finance. Post MBA, I had the fortune of working with IBM and several Fortune 500 companies across various sectors including Manufacturing, Specialty Chemicals, Finance, Insurance, Education, Research & Development and the US Government. After 13 years of experience with them, I started working on the IT group of using multiple channels, which was a unique and fresh concept. I also engaged myself with public speaking and although I don't term myself as a motivational speaker, I do a lot of motivational talk. I also strongly believe that an entrepreneur has to have qualities much beyond the normal service, oriented mindset. I provide them with solutions to make a difference in their lives," says Tarun.

Tarun started his venture of providing IT solutions through multiple channels and has been a founder of a startup called 'Telligent Inc' and the recent one being the iachievegroup.com. This portal of iachieve has a business model that empowers people to unleash their potential and become successful entrepreneurs. An intelligent collaboration of knowledge and experience, they specialize in leveraging the power of Social Media to help individuals establish their own global online businesses.

Tarun never really believed in asking for funds. But why? Is seeking funding by many of us a wrong thing? Does it involve some kind of complications, which could be detrimental?

"I have never believed in asking for money from anybody as I always wanted to stay away from debts and hence, I have self-funded my ventures. In order to ensure that I do not stumble upon any barriers, I started making my bank of savings while I was in a job. Once I began my journey of entrepreneurship, I embarked upon it slowly by infusing it with my savings and with money, I made more money and my journey kept on going," says Tarun.

He further adds, "You know there are people who one fine day get a kick that they need to become an entrepreneur and quit their jobs and then start thinking of what they want to do. I mean, People think entrepreneurship is similar to working from 9 to 5 but it isn't that way, it requires a lot of dedication, a vision, determination and most importantly, an idea to work on. I remember the other day I was called by a young woman who had quit her job recently and she was like, what do I do? How should I get funding? It does not work that way".

Tarun did take the courageous decision of funding his venture with his savings. Here one thing is noteworthy and that is the vision and discipline, which is called for in this kind of funding. Many of us could fail in spite of the vision and that is the challenge.

Tarun has ably managed his savings and earnings, to make what we know today as the iachievegroup.com, a portal for ambitious and wannabe entrepreneurs.

So, let's dig deep, and try and chart out the story behind Tarun's simple yet interesting saga of funding.

"Like I mentioned, I never believed in funding from external sources and hence I started funding from my personal savings and my ventures. The benefits of the of the same were multiple such as no debt and no worries regarding interest, which kept me happy.

Secondly, I was more conscious of using my funds aptly as I had a limited source. It is not as it once you take a debt, you will become careless but since you have a good amount of funds at your disposal, one could become less careful.

Thirdly, as I had my own money, the profit margin also was booked higher in some cases as it gave me leverage of playing with it. I did not have to capture the costs of money.

I never had any experience of disadvantages or demerits and hence, I see no restrictions with self-funding apart from the fact that since you are putting your own funds, you need to be doubly sure of every penny you are spending. So be wise while spending and choose the right platform to spend on," says Tarun.

With Tarun's example and many other such examples, it's no secret that the most popular source of startup financing is the personal savings of the business founder. But while almost everyone will tell you that you must use your personal savings when starting a business, very few people will advise you on the more important question: What percentage of your personal savings should you use? Should you pour all your savings into your budding business? Should you use 50 percent or less? I'm going to offer some tips on how to use your personal savings effectively to get your business off the ground.

As per the wise, a designated amount of your savings must be invested. The most prudent approach is to keep a 'diversified investment portfolio'. This means that you should not invest 100% of your personal savings in any single investment, including your own company - ever.

Investing personal savings in a business is an important milestone. Holding back some savings for a rainy day's needs should not be perceived as any lack of faith in your business prospects. Rather, look at it as a positive confirmation that you can be a shrewd business investor who is out to reduce needless risks at every turn.

Many of us would think, what if I don't end up making money and I lose my savings also? But if you believe the company has a good chance, you must invest your savings, because it's the only logical way to make the finances work!

If you don't think the company has a good chance, you should not work there but save your money because you are wasting your most valuable asset — your time. You could be better off spending time with your family and making a good living. You might argue that you're already putting yourself at risk by working at the company/job, so you should keep your savings as a cushion for your family. But actually you're still doing your family a disfavor, because it's almost impossible for you to earn back the reward on your time.

Of course the value of working at a startup isn't just financial. It's more fulfilling, more exciting, more fun, and nowhere else will you learn as much about as many things. That counts a lot, perhaps even more than the potential for making money!

The example of Don Poffenroth who at age 44 made what some, including his wife, would consider a dubious decision. He invested all of his retirement savings in shares of the startup business Dry Fly Distilling. But seven years later, he has no regrets. Dry Fly is an award-winning micro distillery with 5 employees and $2 million in annual sales.

Dry Fly Distilling is true craft distillery, located in beautiful Spokane, Washington. We produce award-winning vodka, gin, whiskies, and now bourbon using only locally grown grains and botanicals.

Tarun has his own contemplation for not having anyone on board for an investment and has a piece of advice here "By associating with people who share the same moral values and interests as you, you won't have to be constantly trying to live up to their expectations, nor will you have to lower yourself to meet their standards, and thus violate all that you know to be right. Be very selective in whom you choose to associate with. This could determine your path of journey ahead. It is therefore, very detrimental for you to NOT consider this". Tarun has mastered this school of thought and hence became a winner.

He could well be the quintessential person to have his own dreams, and his own means to fund them as well. He decided very early that he would/will not depend on external sources of funding and get his dreams funded with his own money.

This could well trigger a thought in your mind that is that we all have savings and always want to have more savings and more smart money management, which looks easy on the face of it, but it is a concept like a tight water compartment, which only half the world has tried to understand.

Some of Tarun's customer testimonials-

Testimonial from a Project Manager@ Dallas, Texas
What attracted me the most to iAchieveGroup is the quality of people who are already successful in their professional careers, and on top of that, they are working towards a common goal with purpose and passion. It is almost like a secret society of entrepreneurs. I wanted to be in the inner circle of such a powerful network. I have always heard that five years from now, the quality of our lives will be determined by the caliber of people we associate with and the books we read. I am proud to be associated with this incredible organization which has provided me a platform to grow and empower myself to run a successful business.

Testimonial from a student @ Atlanta G
Honesty and integrity is what I saw in the eyes of Tarun Gupta, the founder of iAchieveGroup. I could see he was committed to excellence and infused the same spirit within his organization. I instantly connected to his mission and realized that this was the only platform where I could grow personally and professionally, and also contribute to society at the same time. This is a team where everyone works selflessly, and there is a genuine desire to give while being willing to shed our egos and contribute for a bigger cause. This is a platform that gives you wings to fly and the guidance to turn every dream into a reality.

Testimonial from a SAP Consultant @ Pune, India.
The first thing that attracted me towards iAchieveGroup was its name, which is the very essence of this organization. Each individual associated with it is an achiever and while everyone works as a close-knit team, we also work on accomplishment of our own personal and professional goals. So, while we may be able to realize tangible financial benefits for us individually, the effort that goes in is definitely plural. This means we are never alone in this journey towards becoming a successful entrepreneur. Exciting, result-oriented, intellectual, challenging and never devoid of action – this is a phenomenal team and an ideal business.

He was recently crowned the **"Global ICON of the Month" by Inspiration Unlimited eMagazine.**

So would Tarun recommend this to other entrepreneurs?

"Definitely, but first they need to understand that entrepreneurship is not just an assignment which they have to complete but also a commitment. One must be very planned, focused and clear with what they want to do. Once they are clear, they can then start saving funds as and when they can, and invest on their dream venture. This will give them confidence, a road map and also make them a better entrepreneur," says Tarun.

Tarun says his mission is to provide opportunity, knowledge, motivation and an environment of growth for entrepreneurs to build their own independent business and to encourage a life of excellence built on principles, ethics and right values. Above all, he wants to make a difference by assuming responsibility, taking ownership and adding value to everything he does.

Great!!! Tarun has been very instrumental in providing coaching and mentorship in the areas of Business Ethics and Leadership, Time Management and Wealth

Management to entrepreneurs in India and North America via social media channels, seminars and speaking engagements.

Fund-O- Drama

Funding Technique – Funding through business and own savings

Prerequisites: Well-planned savings plans before you embark on your entrepreneur journey, good idea for entrepreneurship, balanced cost planning to ensure every penny is utilized in the best optimum manner.

Time to fund	Less More
Ease of fund	Low High
Amount	Less More

17

www.alexishaselberger.com

Alexis, a young and dynamic professional with an experience of more than 15 years behind her, is a productivity, time-management and efficiency expert based out of the San Francisco Bay Area. She spent the first 15+ years of her career managing operations and HR at several early-stage startups, where there was always way more to do than people to do it.

Her productivity and time-management systems, techniques, tricks and hacks can be customized to any team, individual or household. Her aim is to help you do all that you want to do, with less effort and less stress.

Most of her work testimonials in the business world have been amazing and great. For instance, Brianna Reynaud, VP the Outcast Agency says about Alexis, "Alexis Haselberger is a tremendous productivity coach. I initially worked with Alexis at a fast-paced startup and she was tasked with helping our small and mighty team boost our productivity. The tools and techniques she offered were invaluable and immediately lifted the sense of anxiety I was feeling about not having enough time to do everything that needed to be done. Her sessions helped me become more focused and calmer, and to this day I routinely draw on the techniques drawn by Alexis."

Hussein Mehanna, Director of Engineering at one of the prestigious platforms says, "I have really enjoyed working with Alexis. Her structured approach allowed me to absorb the techniques and build habits around them. I found the sessions very valuable!"

Alexis services all kinds of clientele such as -

- Individuals with big jobs/lives who are stressed and/or overwhelmed and want to take back control. (Working parents, busy managers/execs, entrepreneurs, etc.)
- Companies/teams who value personal development and/or who want high performance and – check spacing results without employee burnout.
- People who say things like:
    - "Man, I just don't have enough hours in the day!"
    - "I'm so exhausted!"
    - "I've got too much on my plate!"
    - "I have no down-time!"
    - "I feel like I'm failing at work AND home!"

These are some of the examples where Alexis has surpassed her client's expectations and delivered excellent results. And mind you, she has been doing this since many years. But the real question here is not about her success as an entrepreneur but about her passion to begin this. Despite being in a comfortable and good zone, she still decided to start her own journey and become successful at it. The most striking feature about her journey is that she embarked on it despite not having the required funds or should I say, adequate funds. This made her finally bootstrap her venture and ensure that she succeeds.

When I say bootstrap, it only means that she decided to use her personal savings to finance her dream venture and did not blink an eye before doing it.

Most of the time, we all save for our old age, our world tours, our vacations, our desires, and some such things. But here is this one enthusiastic entrepreneur, who used her funds to bootstrap her passion - her venture. Most of us would think twice before taking such huge financial risks so let us know from Alexis her initial thoughts after she decided to bootstrap?

"Well I'm a solo practitioner; it seemed unlikely I'd be able to secure outside funding," says Alexis rather candidly.

She was sure that she may not get her desired funding as the systems here probably do not give her the desired rating to be able to qualify as a promising venture. So, instead of letting her passion die within her, she decided to pursue it and make it happen.

Must appreciate here her willingness and fire to make things happen. As the saying goes, all's well that ends well and Alexis's gamble paid off. Today Alexis has a good number of clients and is successful. The testimonials above prove the same.

A bootstrapped company usually grows through various stages:

1. Beginning Stage: Normally starts with some personal savings, or borrowed or investment money from friends and family, or as a side business. Like it happened in the case of Alexis. She did the same thing to ensure success.

2. Customer-billing cycle received funds Stage: Where money from customers is used to keep the business operating and, eventually, funds growth. This slowly boosts your confidence, builds your customer base and probably then you are ready to jump to the next level of funding for growing your business.

3. Seeking loans Stage: Wherein the entrepreneur must focus on the funding of specific activities, such as improving equipment, hiring staff, etc. At this stage, the company takes out loans or may be even find venture capital, for expansion.

There have been many big and small names in business which began on a small note and scaled up to being one of the most prestigious brands in the world.

They all had humble beginnings with being bootstrapped most of the times and later scaled up to reach new heights. Therefore, it is very important to take that first step and be the success story everyone writes home about. Not doing it or giving it up or being too skeptical about yourself or the service you wish to provide will only mess things up.

So, what does Alexis think could have been the advantage and the disadvantage of her using this kind of funding? To this she says -

1) The primary advantage is that I'm beholden to no one. I make all my own decisions.

2) The disadvantage is that I'm constantly looking for free resources (free software, etc.) and that I don't have much of a marketing budget.

Therefore, what this concludes for us is that having personal savings leaves you in a better position to make your own decisions and eliminates dependency on other modes of securing funds/loans. But on the flip side, Alexis draws attention to the fact that self-funding leaves very little budget for marketing. She further ads, "If I were to open another sole proprietorship, then I would use the same kind of funding and if I were trying to start a larger company, with a staff, with a product instead of a service, then I'd likely seek out outside funding."

That means, for all those who are themselves the product of their business should use this source of funding as here you have minimum risk and you can play around. This can happen when you are a professional with skill sets like coaching in case of Alexis. You may possess skills like Art, Music, Sports, etc. which you could convert into a sole proprietorship and steadily and slowly grow into a business and then may be if need be, remodel into a larger company.

This makes complete sense since I believe that when you deter to take risk, you invite only boredom and an unaccomplished status in life. But here, Alexis took charge and ensured that she adequately saved money to bootstrap her venture. It is difficult, it is challenging at times, but it is rewarding as well to be able to pursue your interest and realize your dream.

So, would she recommend this source of funding to others?

"Yes, of course, but just make sure that you have enough runway to get yourself to a sustainable client-base. Building a paying client base takes time and having some savings and a realistic idea of how long it will take to secure a strong client-base will ensure that the process is not as stressful as it could otherwise be. Also, do whatever you can in your spare time before you quit your job: create your business plan, build your website, etc. Everything that you can do while you still have an income will help you get to your sustainable client-base faster."

Yes, makes sense. One must be planned, draw out the road map and must see what best he or she can do to achieve her /his dreams instead of giving it up. Someone has very rightly said
"Trying is giving an option to failure,
But not trying is ensuring failure."

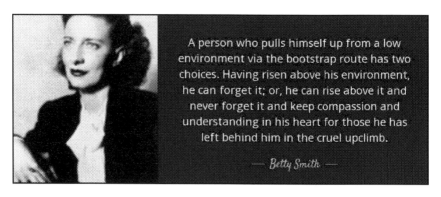

A person who pulls himself up from a low environment via the bootstrap route has two choices. Having risen above his environment, he can forget it; or, he can rise above it and never forget it and keep compassion and understanding in his heart for those he has left behind him in the cruel upclimb.

— *Betty Smith* —

Alexis has already begun her journey well and we are sure with the humble beginnings, she will for sure scale up to new heights and make things happen as she has already been doing it.

Fund-O- Drama

Funding Technique – **Bootstrapping from Personal Savings**

Prerequisites: Personal Savings, well chalked out Plan, Clear Vision. Few customers already working with you.

Time to fund	
	Less More
Ease of fund	
	Low High
Amount	
	Less More

18

Mobitrack

 **MobiTrack Technologies (P) Ltd is a company based out of Bangalore, India** which specializes in Location Based Service for Field Force through Mobile, RFID, NFC, Barcode, Bluetooth, Hybrid apps, Indoor GPS etc. Their objective is to build ecosystem with world's top companies within the product ranges and create unique Product /Marketing and Market in India and other countries. They are also scaling up I mport and Export of Mobile Business Enterprise Applications in 8 Countries and are in talks with various large companies like 3i InfoTech, ICICI Bank, Modi International, Crystal Phosphate LTD, TVS Rubbers, Metropolis Ltd etc and SMB Markets in India.

Founder: Manoj Patel

 Meet Manoj Patel, a promising entrepreneur with degree in Computer Science from Oxford College, Bangalore. He has several years of experience behind him where he has worked for companies like BangaloreIT.co.in as a Senior Relationship/ Engagement Manager and served positions in other companies as well. As the founder and CEO of MobiTrack, Manoj has specialties in Customizing Mobile Application on Location Tracking, Workforce Management System, Sales force Automation, Mobile CRM, Order Management and Service and Distribution Channel.

Imagine you receive an invitation, not for marriage or party but for investing in a startup and in return you are offered to be on their board with a predefined stake sitting with you. To add to the joy, you don't even have to have your grey cells exercised in the day-to-day operations of the company. It's your money that will work for you like a typical financial investment; however, this source could reap you much more than the average earnings of any other investments. You may draw similarities with equity funding where there is a stake offered. But here, the investors who were offered the stake were not someone whom Manoj really knew. He had randomly contacted few of the worthy people who he thought could come on board. It's Interesting and sounds different, but as a matter of fact, this is really very different which has been practiced in realty by MobiTrack.

Manoj Patel, founder, MobiTrack, did this in a very unthinkable fashion. He actually sent out invitations to various target investors inviting them to invest and reap the benefits of being a director and also enjoy the stake. It was as casual as sending out an invitation for one's marriage or engagement.

"We are into customized mobile applications solutions provider business, where we work with various domain areas. We founded the company in 2009 with our savings and started to build on the technology, but there was a stage when we realized that we needed more funds to give it the necessary kick but did not know what and how to do," says Manoj.

MobiTrack is based out of Bangalore and is doing beautifully well for itself. So what transpired them to dig into this kind of an innovative way of procuring funds?

"At that time, I was quite active with the IIM Bangalore (One of the very prestigious colleges in India) and would regularly visit to attend their various seminars and in one such seminar, I met a consultant who sounded me off with this idea, which at the beginning, looked very silly but somehow it just stuck to my mind and would not leave me. I was kind of thinking on it and then *Eureka*… I thought it could be a workable solution. After all, you are being honest with your delivery and in return, are getting the funds. I kept harping on this idea for long and after a lot of discussion and meetings with this consultant and my team members, we, in our minds, had a broader framework set out. The frame work was basically with respect to the offer pattern, the stake to offer for what kinds of amount and so on, and finally we were set for rolling out the invitations," says Manoj.

Manoj planned very naively the idea of having investors on board by offering them equity. The difference he tried to bring in was with the way he did it. We will see that later but for now what we need to understand is that he was trying and having his pie split amongst many investors since basic idea behind equity is the splitting of a pie. When you start something, your pie is really small. You have a 100% of a really small, bite-size pie. But when you take outside investment and your company grows, your pie becomes bigger. Your slice of the bigger pie will be bigger than your initial bite-size pie.

When Google went public, Larry and Sergey had about 15% of the pie each. But that 15% was a small slice of a really big pie.

So in Manoj's case, how did he go about offering his pie to the investors?

"After working out each detail with my team, we freezed on a framework.

We opted for the following –

a) 500,000 USD – investor turns board of director with 5% stake.

b) 1 million usd – investor turns board of director with 10% stake.

c) 2 million USD – investor turns board of director with 20% stake.

d) 3 million usd – investor turns board of director with 30% stake.

We had made it clear that we will have 3 investor board of directors or less depending on investments and obviously, the stake that we offered them was at par with their investment with 5% for 5 lakhs, 10% for 10 lakhs and so on." says Manoj.

Well I would say Manoj was much sorted. He knew probably what he wanted to do. Otherwise, when you are starting a company or are a part of a startup or a key player, some ownership (equity) in the company is usually part of the deal. The founder of a company, if she or he is alone, owns the whole thing. If you are the owner of a business and want to convince somebody with necessary and critical skills to come on board, for your company to succeed, you may need to offer them equity, because you probably can't pay them otherwise. And if you need financing to get your business off the ground, you may need to swap equity for those funds. How much equity should you give away? How much equity should you ask for when you are working for a startup?

Mr. Michael Cradock, Director of Morgan Cradock, a Management consultancy specializing in capital, strategy and people, opines to first agree with your investor on what the potential future valuation might be via reference to other company data that has achieved an exit or is quoted on a stock exchange. He also adds that many entrepreneurs fail to use available data. There are stock exchanges in the UK (AIM) and in the USA (NASDAQ) that provide you with plenty of companies to compare to. You can always discount these valuations to suit your particular case. Once you agree on the future valuation, then you can discuss the existing technology roadmap, risks and options that might open up and what rewards should there be for the risks inherent in the business over the 12 months until the next capital raising round. You then account for any other investments required.

Your goal is to raise large amounts of capital only when you have proven the viability of your business model. No start-up should raise all its capital in one go, otherwise you risk extreme dilution. This is a fact you will have to come to terms with. Your goal now is getting to the next stepping stone and funding round. It's wise to have a capital raising expert on your team who is aligned and is given incentive to raise the capital you need at consecutive rounds so that you can focus on the hard part, developing the technology and getting customers to buy the technology.

Mr. Cradock has indeed put a fair amount of light on the road map to gauge investors but in Manoj's case, why anybody based on, an invitation fund you?

"Today, a lot of people, who look for stable incomes apart from their regular job/work incomes, don't mind taking the risk provided the concept is good. This was my USP. I was sitting on a good concept and hence I could gather the momentum to pitch myself.

Besides, it gives the investor a privilege of being called a director and enjoys some returns also without his involvement. He is just like a silent player and we are the riders who ride on his money and promise him predefined returns.

Secondly, the amount that was asked from each one of them was not running in multiple numbers and hence it was not very cumbersome for them to invest.

Lastly, people start recognizing you, once the word spreads across. This too gives the needed lift to the whole scenario," says Manoj.

Although this is not equity funding by definition, let us still call this one since the operational part of it is more or less same to equity financing. When we compare it to debt financing, there are some major ups when it comes to equity funding since debt accrues interest payable on it.

Let see some of the main differences between Equity and Debt Financing.

Sr. No	Equity Financing	Debt Financing
1	The ownership is offered through means of certain percentage	There is no ownership stake shared.
2	There is no interest payable of debt one has raised	There is interest payable on the amount
3	in Equity financing, there are no set dates as to which one needs to pay an installment compiled of principal and interest factored in it	Debt financing often comes with strict conditions or covenants in addition to having to pay interest and principal at specified dates

We have seen some of the benefits that Manoj had from this kind of funding. Let us also see if any limitations that Manoj feels that this process could have-

'Yes, every coin has 2 sides and so does this. The major drawback or limitation critical to business is that the information of your company and the funds intended to invest, goes through wrong people sometimes and hence this could prove disastrous for you. The startup needs to be a little careful in managing the same.

Two, the process is very tiresome and requires real good energy and presentation to appropriately pitch the concept and the requirement," says Manoj.

What else should we know of this "invitation/equity" route to funding? "Your concept should be earth shattering and your homework on the dynamics of the proposal should be thorough. It should not happen that the investor challenges you in some arena and you are left dumbstruck. Secondly, as mentioned, have a good presentation methodology which will enrich the customer and impress him. This is very vital for success here," says Manoj.

Now that it is almost four years since this jaunt and the rolling out of his venture, what is his take?

"It's been good. Since we managed funding through this route, we are now confident to pitch our proposals to the big VC's and get a mammoth amount for further leveraging our business. Had I not taken this route, I would have been probably still vouching for kickstarting my ambitions," says Manoj.

We saw that this kind of funding was something similar to the equity financing yet it had a flavor of difference. And the difference was the selection of investors randomly.

So how did Manoj actually go about selecting his vendors? Any criteria for selection to invite the right people?

There could be several ways that a startup can attract an equity investor by Manoj's way or generally and send him an invitation to come on board as Manoj did-
- First Know the basics as below-
  a) Why do you need funding?
  b) How much funding will you need?
  c) By when do you need the funding?
- Create an Exit Plan so that there is clarity for investors.
- Solidify your contracts with customers you deal with, to have more appeal in your proposal and boost confidence of the investor.
- Build a product pipeline where the investor knows about the kind of product you dealt with.
- Be organized since this will enhance your reputation in front of the investor.
- Get a realistic valuation so that there are no elements of confusion later. Have a stronger team.

"We know that senior members in the corporate world, startup investors, investment and banking professionals and finally advisories/consultants could be the different categories, to which we float our invitations. These could be the people who would want to invest and retain some stakes in companies," says Manoj.

Will he do it again?

"Yes I will, since it is a good way but this time, in order to not lose much time, I may have a traditional offer of proposing additional stake for the early birds. It may sound like any other retail products on sale offer, but yes, the additional 5 or 10% stake for early birds could shorten my cycle for the right investors. And certainly as a policy decision, I will definitely want to get back to this method for any of my other future dream works," concludes Manoj.

Manoj is an ambitious and determined entrepreneur and its hats off to his ability to trust the equity way of funding a startup. MobiTrack specializes in Location Based Service as mentioned earlier, their core competence is in the space of mobile technology and innovative technology products that exceed client expectations and delight the end user. MobiTrack's rich experience and exposure to various technologies enables them to provide the best technology to the clients. *Their clients are from diverse sectors like Retail, Pharma, Power, Insurance, Automotive and Healthcare. The potential client list tapped by MobiTrack is Rasna International, Onida amongst others.*

Fund-O- Drama

Funding Technique – Invitation to criteria based investors to own stake as a Director.

Prerequisites: Earth shattering concept, very good presentation skills, patience and perseverance.

Time to fund	
	Less More
Ease of fund	
	Low High
Amount	
	Less More

19

Aikon Labs

 Aikon Labs Pvt Ltd is a startup focused on helping to realize ideas. Their product 'Verve' is a solution for tapping ideas within the stakeholders in an Enterprise,

Academic, Researcher or Open communities. Verve enables the Idea to Pilot (I2P) lifecycle, taking ideas through a customer defined innovation process. Verve is a comprehensive innovation management and execution solution that utilizes and engages users with Social Networking tools while helping organizations & institutions with Process, Document and Analytics management throughout the I2P life-cycle. Verve seamlessly plugs into social & professional networks like Facebook & LinkedIn as well as Intranets, Extranets and other web & mobile applications!

Founder: Dilip Thomas Ittyera

 Dilip Ittyera is a die-hard entrepreneur and Evangelist with hands-on involvement in many startups and three decades of experiences - dropouts, failures and a string of pioneering innovations. His specialties are Entrepreneurship, Innovation and Indian Product startups. He has had a fascinating spectrum of experiences within the IT industry spanning three decades. Aikon Labs is the fifth startup that he is involved with. His experience spans both established companies as well as startups, in India and the US. He is the **Founder & Chief Executive Officer of Aikon Labs.** Dilip has been associated with companies like Zensar Technologies as their Chief Innovation Evangelist, and CTO, apart from being Head of Engineering in Calkey Technologies Inc. and many others before embarking on this current venture, Aikon Labs.

Have a home? If yes, you have fair chances of getting funding for your entrepreneurship dreams.

The loan, which we will talk about here, will be a kind of loan which will enhance your chances if you have a home. The loan type I am talking about here is a revolving credit line. Yes, a revolving credit line, a facility which enables you to tread your path of entrepreneurship and also gives you the opportunity to fulfill your dreams. This is exactly what was done by our next entrepreneur, Dilip. He was instrumental in finding a unique way of funding but only after running pillar to post and after sweating it out did he get the golden opportunity of getting his funds sanctioned.

Revolving credit is a type of credit that does not have a fixed number of payments, in contrast to installment credit. Credit cards are an example of revolving credit used by consumers. Then there are the corporate revolving credits facilities, which are typically used to provide liquidity for a company's day-to-day operations.

"I founded Aikon labs in 2009 end and started operations in 2010. As a typical and traditional means, I started it with my own funds and scaled up my business from scratch.

After I started my shop and scaled it up, I required the desired funds to further expand my business and hence I tried going for the traditional business loans, those which are offered by banks but the same was not to be for me since my startup was into making software products and I wanted a little less stringent loan." says Dilip.

After a lot of struggle, the idea of a revolving credit line struck Dilip and he decided to pursue it.

Revolving credit line is surely a good option and a nice way of funding your startup. With several benefits like lower interest rate, withdrawal of money at your own pace etc it is a practical option for bootstrapping a startup. In other words, a revolving credit, as mentioned above, is considered as a credit card, which enables you to use the cash at your disposal as per your choice.

The same revolving credit line becomes a feasible option if you have a home owned by you as it is then called as a **Home Equity Line of Credit.**

Dilip further continues, "During my career, I learnt the concept of the revolving credit line. It is also called as a **HELOC,** or **Home Equity Line of Credit**, a type of facility that allows a borrower to open up a line of credit using their home as collateral.

It differs from a conventional home loan for several different reasons. The main difference is that a HELOC is simply a line of credit that allows a homeowner to borrow up to a pre-determined amount set by the mortgage lender, whereas with a conventional mortgage the amount borrowed is the total amount financed and you have to pay EMIs for the defined tenure.

I thought of exploring this idea as I was sure that in India also, something similar exists, although many banks refrain from doing so."

So what could be the sum up of a Revolving Credit Line? Let's find out-

A revolving credit line basically allows you to avail up to a certain amount against a property. Since I had the home loan as well, I got the revaluation of my home done. The appreciation in value ensured that a percentage of the balance amount, after accounting for my home loan, was made my revolving credit line. The usual home loan tenure is about 15-20 years and often the value of your home increases after a few years into the home loan disbursal. This period also gives the bank a fair idea about your repayment track record, and if that record is good, it increases your eligibility for getting the facility sanctioned.

How did Dilip manage the revolving credit line?

"I had taken a home loan to buy my house. Over a few years, the value of the house had appreciated. Hence, I thought if I could get a credit facility sanctioned by a bank based on the increased value of the home, I could pursue my dream of undertaking the entrepreneurship journey. Therefore, with documents and my business plan, I visited many nationalized and private banks but they all turned me down. After a lot of running around, I finally knocked on the door of the Saraswat Cooperative Bank and after initial discussions, they agreed to go for the processing of the revolving credit line," says Dilip.

Dilip did something which may not be heard of much. This may not be a very popular route to funding as banks refrain offering such services and it is by and large offered to a customer. But, since Dilip was an existing home loan customer the game was more in his favor. Having said that, it is the sheer hard work and passion displayed by Dilip, which enabled him to get the loan sanctioned!

So how does this loan work?

"For example, suppose you have a house worth 10 million USD as per market valuation and you have a home loan of 2million USD on it. Now the disposable amount that you could avail is 8 million USD. But the banks retain a margin and offer the balance as the revolving credit line, so, for instance in this case, they may retain a margin of 3 million USD and offer you the balance of 5 million USD as a revolving credit line," says Dilip.

The extra benefits

Revolving credit line home loans or HELOC as we have seen, unlike loans against property, are extended even to people having their existing home loan. The following are the extra benefits of Revolving Credit Line.

A) OD (Overdraft) & such Loan facilities from a co-operative bank would normally cost less than that from private banks.

B) The customers have the choice to draw the money from their account as and when the need arises and interest is charged only on the utilized amount.

C) One can remit the revenues that you earn into the facility thereby reducing the outstanding amount & the interest payable

D) The processing fees of this kind of facility is also very less. It is pocket friendly for the entrepreneur.

E) The tenure of the credit facility is renewed by the bank based on a review of your business.

Lender consider factors like value of the property, outstanding home loan repayment history and repayment capacity before approving the loan.

An interesting aspect of a revolving credit line loan is that it can be utilized for businesses as working capital.

There have been many instances where one can think of where the revolving credit line in ideal circumstances could be of benefit.

Let's take a quick example.

Let's say that you have a credit card with a 1000 USD. You charge 200 USD over the course of the month, which leaves you with available credit of 800 USD by the end of the month.

If you pay off the full balance at the end of the month, then you are back to having 1000 USD in borrowing power on your credit card. This is revolving credit.

An example of non-revolving credit is a car loan. With a car loan, you have a set EMI (Equated Monthly Installments) that needs to be paid until the loan is paid off. Once the loan is paid off, there is no more credit available, and your loan is closed.

So with that as an example, we can understand the nuances of a revolving credit line! Let us see how Dilip's experience was in using the revolving credit line-

"I feel revolving credit lines have various benefits:

Firstly, you are able to bootstrap your business based on the mortgage of your house.

Secondly, cooperative banks like, the Saraswat bank have low interest rates.

Thirdly, with a revolving credit line, you are charged interest only for the amount consumed by you, something similar to the cash credit facility," says Dilip.

Great! So Dilip has given a good insight as to the benefits of a revolving credit line. Let us dig deeper and see what more a revolving credit line can offer.

The banks these days are offering attractive revolving credit lines for customers against their property and can be used to fulfill their business needs. Dilip used the proceeds from the revolving credit line for his entrepreneurship dreams.

The key features of a revolving credit line are:

1. Easy access to funds, with most revolving credit facilities offering cheque books, plastic cards, Internet and phone banking and a range of transactions

2. Withdraw up to your credit limit at any time

3. Use the available funds in your revolving credit facility to bootstrap your business

4. Reduce your overall monthly repayments by consolidating your debts into a low rate credit facility

5. Ability to minimize your monthly interest charges by depositing all of your income into the account and withdrawing as you need it

These were some of the characteristics of a revolving credit line. The biggest advantage I see in this kind of loan is that you can immediately meet your business requirements. Had Dilip chosen to tread the path of other loan options, he would have spent more time on negotiating and driving them. End result would have been the delay in realization of the business growth.

In totality, a good source of funding, but hold on, there could be certain shortcomings also?

"Yes, a major one being the fate of losing your house if your calculation goes wrong!

And, to do this, one needs consent from the family as well. The Family is of prime importance and since this is the shelter for all the family members, their approval is also important.

With some risks associated with it, one needs to really and seriously think through this and then take a call and be careful to use it wisely," says Dilip.

Yes, it is true. The funding is a good one, but involves certain amount of risk if you have a home and you have taken a loan against it. We all know that once a home is mortgaged to any kind of loan, we are always at higher risk, especially if that is the only shed we have to embrace ourselves with grace.

God, this is critical, so would Dilip use this source of funding again if need be?-

'Yes, I would do it again if I ever need to do it in future, but this time I will go to the cooperative bank directly instead of wasting my time behind other banks," says Dilip.

He further continues "I also strongly recommend this method to others but with a word of caution. Firstly, please do not use this source of funds if you are only dilly dallying with the idea of entrepreneurship and are not serious as this could lead to serious consequences.

Secondly, as part of this process, make a business plan, which will help you as well as give the banks a good idea of what your plans are," concludes Dilip.

Terrific guts and I would say a very different approach to funding.

In the end, we leave you with an infographic on how 'Verve', the product of 'Aikon' works:

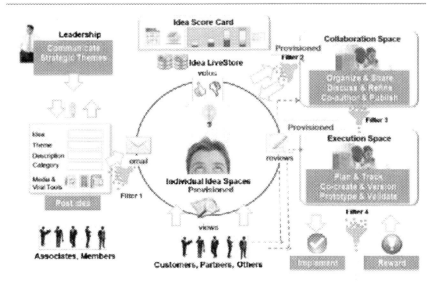

Fund-O- Drama

Funding Technique –Revolving credit lines against property

Prerequisites: Preferably owning a property and calculated risk taking ability.

Time to fund	Less More
Ease of fund	Low High
Amount	Less More

20

Knowlarity

Knowlarity came to life in 2009, when Ambarish Gupta realized that business telephony in India was a revolution in the making. It was a time when expensive and archaic on-premise telephone systems dominated business telephony for the few that could afford it. Small and medium enterprises who did not want to make such investments on infrastructure had to contend with complex and manual routing of their incoming call volume.

For those who wonder what "Knowlarity" means: it is a confluence of "Knowledge" and "Singularity". Their goal is to achieve that inflection point where their products approach near—human intelligence.

Founder: Ambarish Gupta

Ambarish Gupta is the CEO and Founder of Gurgaon-based cloud telephony startup Knowlarity Communications. A graduate in Computer Science from the Indian Institute of Technology, Kanpur, Ambarish also holds an MBA from Carnegie Mellon University, USA. A technocrat at heart, he believes technology holds much potential for changing how the world does business.

Ambarish started his career as a researcher for the Fraunhofer Institute for Computer Graphics in Germany before joining software major EFI. He has also worked with a consulting firm McKinsey & Company as Senior Associate, and in 2009, founded Knowlarity, which provides business telephony software to some of the world's leading corporations.

In his spare time, Ambarish can be found reading, listening to music, or tending to his garden. Extremely environmentally and socially aware, Ambarish believes advances in communication technology can help future generations minimize their impact on the planet, while allowing them to lead more rewarding and fulfilling lives.

As CEO of Knowlarity, Ambarish has used his excellent networking and people skills to gather together a talented and dedicated team that is responsible for the world's best cloud telephony solutions. He believes in leading from the front, and is always available for advice – or a friendly conversation – to any member of the Knowlarity family.

Knowlarity! Heard of Similarity but what is Knowlarity?

Ambarish explains, 'it's a combo of Knowledge and Singularity. Singularity originates from the mathematical concept of multiplying the output with a given input. For example, when an atomic bomb is hit, it bursts into multiple atoms and each atom further multiplies into many more atoms. Similarly, here too we combine knowledge and singularity to give you multiple usages with set inputs. In this case, the super fax machine and the super receptionist machine helps you get organized. These are some of the machines that make life simpler and easier for you".

In the words of Mr. George Bull, National Chair of Professional Practices Group, non-bank external finance is still in the minority for most firms. Some will be able to secure third-party funding for specific client assignments. Others may succeed in attracting external equity investors. Both categories of finance come at a price and, despite the stated interest of private equity funds, it would be an exaggeration to say that external money is pouring into the professions. This could be because the firms do not have compelling use for the money (compelling to the investor, that is) or the management and/or the structure to deliver the vision.

In addition to inter-generational issues within firms, there may also be dilemmas for external investors. Without a doubt, funders prefer proven business models. However, with the pace of change increasing in all professions and firms under real pressure to move to business models that deliver client services in new ways, the very degree of innovation, which may be attractive in the marketplace can be off-putting to investors.

While for many of us, acquiring any kind of funding is a herculean task, Ambarish notched not one but two successive deals, raising in total 8.5 Million USD from Angel funding, and VC funding, from none other than Sequoia Capital.

But why would an organization need funding from two places, especially when the money is coming from two mammoth companies?

Let's ask the man himself. So how did the funding happen?

"I was fortunate to have a robust idea that helped me garner angel funding and also venture capital funding from the leading VC funders, Sequoia Capital," says Ambarish.

Ambarish raised 2 million USD from Angel Investors and nearly 6.5 million USD from Sequoia, sequentially.

"We started in 2009, and in approx. 4 years, we had a work force of about 250 people," says Ambarish proudly.

So why the first round of funding from Angels?

"We wanted to scale our operations first because we knew we would require bigger money later. And so, to scale ourselves optimally, we decided to go for angel investment, in which the expectations aren't as high. It's mainly just about the core team that will manage the show. As very few people have the required backup of funds, it makes sense to first scale it up with angel investment," says Ambarish.

"Once we scaled up, we sought VC funding and were fortunate enough to receive it from Sequoia Capital," he adds.

This is interesting, as here we see a nice strategy wherein this kind of funding could probably have. What I envisage is the smart way of working since in Angel funding as voiced by Ambarish, there are not too many of those deadlines or expectations and so there is always a breather for the startup to perform vis-à-vis VC funder who always have certain strict guidelines and deadlines in place.

Before we proceed ahead and for our common understanding, let's understand what Angel funding and Venture capital means.

Angel investors are often retired entrepreneurs or executives, who may be interested in angel investing for reasons that go beyond pure monetary returns. These include the kind of people who want to keep abreast of current developments in a particular business arena, mentoring or coaching another generation of entrepreneurs, and making proper use of their experience and networks on a less than full-time basis.

Going further, Angels typically invest their own funds, unlike venture capitalists who manage the pooled money of others in a professionally-managed fund. Although typically reflecting the investment judgment of an individual, the actual entity that provides the funding may be a trust, business, limited liability company, investment fund, or other vehicle.

On the other hand, Venture capital (VC) is financial capital provided to early-stage, high-potential, high risk, growth startup companies. The venture capital fund earns money by owning equity in the companies it invests in, which usually has a novel technology or business model in high technology industries, such as biotechnology, IT and software. The typical venture capital investment occurs after the seed funding round as the first round of institutional capital to fund growth (also referred to as Series A round) in the interest of generating a return through an eventual realization event, such as an IPO or trade sale of the company. Venture capital is a subset of private equity. Therefore, all venture capital is private equity, but not all private equity is venture capital.

Obtaining venture capital is substantially different from raising debt or loan from a lender. Lenders have a legal right to interest on a loan and repayment of the capital, irrespective of the success or failure of a business. Venture capital is invested in exchange for an equity stake in the business. As a shareholder, the venture capitalists return is dependent on the growth and profitability of the business. This return is generally earned when the venture capitalist "exits" by selling its shareholdings when, the business is sold to another owner.

Coming back to Ambarish, what was his thought or what he thinks, the real worth of a combo funding like this?

"To begin with, it's easier to convince angel investors. Like I mentioned before, they primarily look at the core team working on the project, their background and capability. VCs look beyond this. They also inspect the business idea, its scalability, the expected output and other such parameters," says the entrepreneur.

"A combination of angel and VC funding makes sense for a business like ours where the chances of getting a VC funding in the initial phase is slim. But once you scale up your operations with angel funding, it's easier to get VCs to invest," he adds.

The combo ensures you get proper rounds of funding.

Secondly the influx of VC funding ensures professional approach of your company. They are brutal about the reality and hence one is constantly on the radar to perform better. They are result driven and hence you are on your toes performing and proving good results.

Lastly, the VC funding takes up a chunk of your equity based on the valuation of your company and hence they help you network in bridging your gaps, which may have occurred in your operations like marketing, technology, etc".

Ok, that could be a parameter to pitch to the VC. Since you got the breather to grow large with the adequate funds required by you, you are ready to now play on a bigger field for which you can now approach the VC. But in my opinion, this also largely depends on your goal that you may have set out for your company. The goal is very ambitious, yes, there could be this VC funding, which can empower you to accelerate past others with, of course, a plan of action in place.

Moreover, if you think deeper, the two rounds of successive funding let you get strong on your foot. It allows you to form your systems and procedures and establish the same.

It can also prove beneficial to establish your product in market and get a good deal over negotiation with your suppliers.

It could therefore be wise to go in for a combo mode of funding phase wise, which Ambarish did.

But there could be some risks also. There are always 2 sides to a coin. Undoubtedly the benefits are tremendous but what about the risks that come with it. Let us understand if Ambarish has had any risks, which he feels relevant.

"Definitely, there are some risks. One is the possibility that you could lose the chance to scale up your operations after the angel funding. You may also have to give a huge chunk of equity to the VC, which has its risks too and requires a lot of operational and decision-making power from you. Lastly, since they (angels or VC) are on board, they may take control of the company and its decisions," says Ambarish.

Let us also have an independent look at some other risks of Angel and VC funding-

Angel Investing Risks-

1) They usually prefer to continue creating new ventures but after having done first one or two ventures, they do not normally like to take executive roles / CEO positions. They, therefore seek to participate as a financial investor, provide strategic inputs and sometimes even provide operational direction to founders / entrepreneurs who are starting up.

2) Angel investments are of the highest risk category in an investor's portfolio but also provide for the highest gain when investments succeed. Hence, to reduce the risk on his investments, an angel typically invests in a number of ventures so that he spreads risks as he knows that only a few of his investments will give him a bumper return, but enough to cover the losses of all his other angel investments and give a good return to his overall portfolio.

3) To further mitigate the risk, he co-invests with other angels as that helps him to initially invest a lower amount as well as the venture gets its complete round of investment from the group of angels. Hence, angel groups start to get formed and collective investments, leveraging each other's domain expertise and networks.

VC Funding Risks-

1) Securing a deal with VC can be a long and complex process.

2) Even if you get through the business negotiation stage, you will have to pay the legal and accounting fees whether or not you are successful in securing funds.

3) You will have to agree to certain limitations as a part of the deal.

4) There could always be a level of scrutiny you will always be put under for your performance related parameters.

Fantabulous! A combo of Angel and VC funding. Would he repeat this funding combo-?

"Definitely, it has proved beneficial for me. But the next time I go for this kind of funding, I will be careful with a few aspects.

A, I will have a proper valuation of my company. Many times, the valuation of the company is underrated by VCs and if you are successful at convincing them, the right valuation could prove beneficial for you.

B, I went with a professional and reputed VC and not just anyone who promised me good returns. It's very important to have the right VC.

C, I would ensure the VC gets substantial equity as this would help discipline my company, ensuring that it doesn't lose focus," says Ambarish.

Kudos! A first of its kind story in this edition with a great combo of Angel and VC funding.

The successive planning of acquiring an Angel funding first and slowly growing to the VC funding level is indeed a nice and better way of acquiring funds. It enables you to get established first and then take that leap to your awaited ambitions.

Knowlarity brings you the best in business telephony. Using the Knowlus cloud telephony platform, their products allow businesses, startups, and other organizations to stay connected 24x7. Whether you're a startup looking for an affordable way to reach out to investors or a global giant seeking to unify your marketing and customer service campaigns, they have the right solution for you.

Awards and Recognition for Knowlarity-

TiE Lumis Entrepreneurial Excellence 2013.

Aegis Graham Bell Award 2011

Best Innovative Emerging Technology 2011

Fund-O- Drama

Funding Technique – **Combo of Angel investors and VC funding sequentially**

Prerequisites: A robust business idea, a good management team, a high octane business plan.

Time to fund	Less More
Ease of fund	Low High
Amount	Less More

21

Brainvisa Technologies

Brainvisa Technologies was founded by four first-time entrepreneurs as an online test prep company in 2000. However, when it did not find traction, it moved to eLearning where it found much more success and, at its peak was considered the top three eLearning companies of India. It worked with a large number of Fortune 500 companies across US, Europe and Australia. In 2007, it was acquired by a Bangalore based KPO and was later merged with the parent company. Its success was attributed to its relentless pursuit of quality and its unwillingness to do cheap and poor quality work. After the acquisition, the promoters moved out and started their own separate ventures, which are doing very well.

Co-Founder: Vikas Kumar

Vikas is one of the few guys in technology who comes from commerce background. He was one of the first non-technology guys to be hired by Infosys Technologies. In Infosys, he quickly made his name as a tech wizard. In 2000, along with his friend from his MBA days and two other first time entrepreneurs, he set up Brainvisa Technologies. Using his technology skills, he built various eLearning products allowing Brainvisa to compete at a global level. After his ten year stint at Brainvisa, he went back to his original passion of helping startups in Technology and strategy. Today, with his wife, he runs SMEJoinup.com a network for Startups and SMEs. (Small and Medium Enterprises)

India is a very conservative and less risk-taking country in terms of funding. Most investors look for safe investments rather than risky investments even if the returns are lower. Therefore investments at concept level or on paper are very rare. And that of first time entrepreneurs rarer still. So, when Vikas tells me that he did exactly this in his first venture, Brainvisa Technologies, I am obviously intrigued and decided to pursue this further.

Pre Revenue Companies getting funded by VCs in India is the exception and not the norm. Even in the early stage, funds less than 10% of their portfolio invested in Pre revenue companies (From Mukund Mohan's Blog). When Vikas and his band went to the investors, they were, what is known in investor parlance, at a concept level. In India, Institutional Investors very rarely invest at a concept level. Most of the funding at this level comes from typically friends and family.

In 2000, Vikas and three other dreamers made an ambitious dream in the education space. To take coaching for various entrance exams like CAT, GMAT online. Remember at that time all coaching was offline since the entrance exams was also written. They created a basic presentation of their idea, stuck in some graphs and started approaching various VCs. In their second attempt, they struck gold when Infinity Ventures decided to invest in them. In a couple of months or so, the deal was done and the first cheque came in.

In about a year, they were all set with their online platform, which they called TestMate. It had support for Adaptive Learning and could simulate Progressive Exams like GMAT. In about a year and a half, with most of the money gone in creating the platform and the content, they realized that it was a dud. The sales were next to negligible as nobody was interested in learning online. With less than a month's run rate in their account, they decided to switch gears and get into eLearning. Luckily they were able to pick up a couple of projects from India. Armed with this confidence, they foraged into US and UK and soon became one of the top 3 companies in eLearning in India.

So with an idea, which, in hindsight, does not seem so great, how were Vikas and his gang able to pick up funding on paper?

"The biggest thing an investor is looking at when you just have a piece of paper is the team," says Vikas. "At a concept level, the investor has very little to go by, so to him, the team is really important and we had done a lot of homework on that. Unlike most of the founding teams, which are basically four friends coming together, we did not know each other. We had formed our team not out of friends but of different skillsets. So while I had a Technology background, Supam was from marketing, Nitin from operations and Anand from finance. We had a diverse skillset and could show strength in all disciplines. This held us in good esteem with the Investors."

So if you are seriously contemplating raising funds at a concept level, make sure your team really rocks. Moreover credentials and background also matter. Vikas' team had three IIM alumni and one IITian. When you have very little to show in terms of experience, pedigree matters a lot. Most investors in India have a respect for IIM and IIT (2 prestigious educational institutes of India known worldwide) alumni. In fact, there are a number of funds, which unofficially only fund IIT/IIM Alumni. So when you are going for funding at a concept level, make sure you have a convincing team backing you up. Four friends, fresh out of college is not the way to go if you are serious about raising funds on a few PowerPoint slides.

Was your past experience important when you were raising funds for your venture? I ask Vikas.

He scratches his head trying to remember those times. "Well, while we did not have long years of experience, our diverse skills again stood out in our past experience. Supam was with a marketing experience, having worked with Pepsi and then a Goa based private company. Anand had finance experience with ICICI Bank. Nitin was handling operation for a team in CITI Bank, while I was with Infosys in technology. Again the experience substantiated our stand of having a diverse team. Investors like such teams, which are working across different companies in different roles. So they bring a rich set of experiences with them. Typically, investors are used to seeing four people quitting a company and starting a venture."

I see Vikas harping on the team and their skill set again. With little to show at a concept level, Investors tend to fall back on the basic theory that a team with a varied skill set tends to do better than a team with similar skill sets. Even in hard core technology companies, Investors tend to prefer teams, which also come with some marketing skills.

So is it only the team or is the idea also relevant when you raise funds at the concept level?

"Well, I won't say the exact idea is important, I would say the space is. Spaces which are new in nature will have a greater chance of getting funded on paper. An unexplored field where the investor is keen to invest in is ideal because the investor does not have many choices and there is very little comparable data. Moreover he cannot find seasoned entrepreneurs in that space. Education in 2000 was an unknown entity with very few attempts to take education online. Most entrepreneurs do not get funded on paper because they are flogging the same dead horse. If you cannot show the investor a running business, at least show him an exciting futuristic idea. Show him the same dead horse and he feels that other existing companies are just too ahead in the game. Also remember that Investors are human. Everybody wants to claim that they identified the next Facebook or Google. So, at a concept level, glamour of the space is key. Even if the idea does not look like a billion dollar idea, the space at least should."

> Recently, I have seen an interesting demand by investors when they invest at a concept or pre-revenue level. Even when the company is in a non-technology field, investors want to see a hard core tech guy in the core team. Not a project lead, not an analyst, but a solid code level guy. With most companies requiring a Website, Online Marketing, Social Media and SEO, Investors feel that any team is incomplete without a tech guy. So if you are contemplating raising funds at a concept level, make sure you have a solid Tech guy with good pedigree in your core team. A degree from IIT would surely help.

Any challenges when you already have cash in the bank?

Vikas smiles. "The funny thing that happens when you get funded on paper, is you start thinking of yourself as the cat's whiskers. And you start taking money for granted. We made the same mistake – we hired costly and over experienced resources, spent money left and right and generally blew away more money than was required. What could be done with maybe a five to six member team, we hired twenty. Like a large software company, we built a tech team with layers of developers, testers and project managers. We only came to our senses when we woke up one day and saw the bank account empty. Up-front money makes you bloated, and entrepreneurship is all about being lean. We were very lucky to have survived. We saw many other companies burning money in the same way till oblivion."

"My advice to any entrepreneurs raising money at a start level would be to put half the money they raise in a locker and throw away the key. Build a small team with freshers or little experience, focus on creating your product rather than managing your team and use the money only when you are ready with the product. If not anything, you will have half the money for trying out something else in case your product fails."

"The other big challenge is equity distribution and salaries. Typically, in such scenarios you end up dividing the shares proportionately like we did and draw equal salaries. However, we quickly learned that this is quite a stupid approach and we re-calibrated the salaries based on the roles we were playing. I have seen a number of companies go down because of this challenge. Equity needs to be divided based on the value, which the team members bring, rather than a mathematical formula. While equal distribution looks great in the short term, eventually it creates discord among the partners and leaves them dissatisfied. In- house fighting among partners is so common in concept level companies, that it is not even funny."

Well it's not all roses. So would you raise funds again on paper for another venture? I ask as a matter of routine.

"No" says Vikas to my amazement. "Not if I can help it. The biggest problem with raising paper money is that you have no bargaining power. You tend to give away a large part of your company and are left with little. This is what happened with us. And after some years, with more rounds of funding, you have very little left and no incentive to continue running the company. We also fell into this trap and finally, with little incentive, we decided to sell out when we could have gone places."

Last question before I sign off; Would you recommend it to other investors?

"Sure", Vikas says, "it is a great way as long as you pick up a small amount in the beginning. Do not pick up capital to survive for three years. Just raise enough to build your product so that you dilute as little equity as possible. Also in cases where you are into risky and unexplored spaces, it makes sense to pick up early funds before the market gets cluttered and the risks become obvious. If you want to explore this option, then make sure that you have taken effort to form a great team with good credentials. Also, it is getting tougher to get funded on paper so don't lose hope. Keep trying out various investors till you get the initial capital."

Fund-O- Drama

Funding Technique – Funding on paper from financial investors or HNIs.

Prerequisites: Great team with super credentials, an idea in a relatively unexplored space

Time to fund	▢▢▢▢
	Less More
Ease of fund	▢▢▢
	Low High
Amount	▢
	Less More

22

Circuit Sutra Technologies

 Circuit Sutra Technologies is an Electronics System Level (ESL) design IP and services company, which specializes in design and verification of Electronics Systems with focus on Semiconductor Chips. Its core competencies include Virtual Platform development, High Level Synthesis and Embedded software development, using Virtual Platforms. Circuit Sutra has a worldwide customer base, which ranges from top 10 Semiconductor companies to the Fabless companies.

Founder: Umesh Sisodia

 Umesh Sisodia, the founder and President of Circuit Sutra is a BTech in Electronics and Telecommunications from Sant Longowal Institute of Engineering and Technology, Punjab. Umesh, after passing out from College, worked for Semiconductor Complex Ltd, a public sector company and Cadence Design Systems, a USA based company, before venturing into his business of semiconductors. Umesh was very sure that one day, he would venture into his own set up and amazingly the timeline on which he decided to do so matched perfectly with his vision. 'Yes, in the year 2000, I was sure that by 2005, I would start my own venture and I did!" said Umesh.

Umesh worked in the semiconductor industry for close to 8 years and by the end of 2005 he decided to form what is today called Circuit Sutra Technologies. So how did the funding happen? Which was the biggest turnaround for Umesh?

"It all happened in the year 2012 when Circuit Sutra was financed as an equity investor by Amity Innovation Incubator. Since the deal was confidential and is bound by contract, we may not be able to reveal the figures here but the deal changed the scale of Circuit Sutra."

The Amity Innovation Incubator is a startup incubator. In the past few years, there has been a surge of Incubators and Accelerators. As per internet articles, there are currently over fifty incubators in India. A number of Incubators are also run by Universities and are primarily run as nonprofit organizations. Amity Incubator of Amity University, CIIE of IIM Ahmedabad, TBIU of IIT Delhi and NSRCEL of IIM Ahmedabad, just to name a few.

But this was not going to be easy as the company being formed in 2005 went through a lot of ups and downs, which obstructed Umesh to reach his company goal he had set out so blissfully for himself.

Umesh, like many of us invested his savings from all those 8 years of perspiration. Umesh says, 'I had made some savings by the end of 2005 and with that investment I started Circuit Sutra.'

For the first one and a half years, there was not much movement happening. Umesh confirms, "Yes, it took us about 1.5 years to identify the technology domain in which we could build a big company. We developed expertise in this technology domain and started getting small projects."

A small turnaround came for Umesh when he received seed funding from **Science and Technology Entrepreneur's Park. The Science & Technology Entrepreneurs Park (STEP)** programme was initiated to provide a re- orientation in the approach to innovation and entrepreneurship involving education, training, research, finance, management and the government. STEP creates the necessary climate for innovation, information exchange, sharing of experience and facilities and opening new avenues for students, teachers, researchers and industrial managers to grow in a trans- disciplinary culture, each understanding and depending on the other's inputs for starting a successful economic venture. STEPs are hardware intensive with emphasis on common facilities, services and relevant equipment's. It's a Government of India initiative.

"We received USD 2.5 million from STEP in the form of equity with a buy back clause and that added some force to our venture, as then it propelled us to venture out for larger avenues," says Umesh.

So how was it like for Umesh to have been funded by STEP?

"It was certainly good and they had an arrangement with us for shares buy back, wherein we would buy back the shares from them once the valuation of the company reached a substantial level. So, after we absorbed their funds and grew, we ended up paying 6.5 million USD as the buyback offer. This happened because STEP and we were not coming to a common understanding of a valuation of the company and hence STEP thought this would be the best way to close them," says Umesh.

However, the major push came when Umesh joined Amity University's Incubation center and allowed Amity to operate out of their premise.

"We shifted our base to Amity incubation center by end 2008 where we had by then completed 3 years of operation after formation. We took up their incubation center to align our infrastructural requirements since they had a bigger place and to leverage on a good startup atmosphere," says Umesh.

One of the biggest advantages of going for incubation is the availability of infrastructure at virtually no cost. This not only brings down the cost of operations significantly, but also allows you to get your business up and running very fast. Many of the incubators also provide support beyond infrastructure in terms of technology and common HR and Admin. This brings down the cost further and also gives you access to quality teams, which you would not be able to afford otherwise.

Many of the incubators have also become great co-working spaces. With many entrepreneurs working out of the same premise, there is a lot of outsourcing of work among the teams themselves. Also there is a higher energy in these incubators as all the incubators work together to achieve similar goals. Incubators like Amity and Investopad have now become great places to work in as you interact with likeminded entrepreneurs.

But destiny seemed to have other plans for Umesh, as the Lehman Brothers Crisis hit the world and Umesh too was a victim of its bang. "Our projects came to a still all of a sudden and there was quite a lot of trepidation of the future. Somehow we managed the situation and pulled on for 2 years", says Umesh.

Unfortunately, Umesh had just started growing his company when this lightning struck, but an undeterred Umesh continued with building and scaling his internal resources and strengths.

Amity connected Umesh to SIDBI (Small Industries Development Bank of India) where he received an unsecured debt of 90 lakhs. "Yes, we were short, listed by Amity and were the first company in that phase to get funded for the same", says Umesh.

SIDBI had initiated the Startups Assistance Scheme, which benefitted companies like Circuit Sutra. This round of funding enabled Umesh to bag projects of quality and consistency.

Incubators not only bring funds of their own but because of their tie-up with various other bodies, they are able to help garner additional bridge rounds. SIDBI also prefers to put funds through incubators like Amity since the due diligence process can be short circuited significantly.

"By 2010, we were able to get some of the top 10 Semiconductor companies as our customers," smiles Umesh.

Indeed, that was good since Circuit Sutra had customers like Texas instruments, USA and Nikon, Japan.

Post this came the real turnaround for Circuit Sutra and that was the funding by Amity themselves under their Incubation Center model, with direct equity in the company.

"Till last year, we were providing only services and then we realized that we should upscale ourselves to build intellectual property portfolio. Thus, from last year itself, we started investing and developing intellectual property", says Umesh.

Amity supported Circuit Sutra in this process by providing the necessary funds. "Yes, the funding from Amity Incubator played a crucial role in transforming the company from a plain services company to the IP based solutions company." Says Umesh.

So how does the entire thing of Amity Incubation go about deciding its stake etc.

Umesh Says, "The equity percentage and the rentals, if any, depend upon the growth potential, stage of the startup, risk involved and are subject to mutual discussions between the startup and the Incubator Management".

So what benefits did Umesh experience from Amity's Incubator funding?

Umesh says, "There are a couple of them. One is the pure equity fund that came our way, which enhanced the credibility of the company. Second, we could, as a team (Amity and Circuit Sutra) come to a common valuation of the company without too many terms and conditions".

"Third, since we had an equity investor with us, we now became more bankable for other investors to trust us and invest in us. This brings in the confidence in a new investor for a Venture Capitalist to have faith and further provide us funding."

Umesh is so supportive of this kind of funding that he believes that there aren't any disadvantages of this kind of funding.

"Yes, I do not find any cons. It is pure equity funding and hence I am happy," says Umesh.

So, does Umesh think he would like to go for this kind of funding again?

"Yes, why not! Although we have already surpassed the requirement of small seed or angel fund, given that now we would hit a bigger requirement soon to scale up. But given a chance, I would certainly opt for it and also strongly recommend it to others."

Apart from Amity, Umesh is also gung ho about the other two sources - the STEP and the SIDBI funding.

"STEP and SIDBI did play a crucial role in Circuit Sutra's life and all our funding came at 3 stages of my business and at every stage, they helped us restructure and grow. For STEP, we could not arrive at a common valuation and had to make a buy back arrangement since a common valuation could not be worked out. Other than this, there were no real challenges that we had with STEP. For SIDBI too, it was a pleasure and there were no real challenges. We had a repayment option after 3 years and our EMI would go on for 4 years after the first 3 years were over", says Umesh.

Umesh is very happy that the 3 kinds of funding came at 3 different stages, the best being the Amity Incubation Center, which helped Circuit Sutra the most.

So what would Umesh, after experiencing the Amity's Incubation center funding advice the reader?

"I would say always negotiate and cross-check that there are no such terms and conditions which could compromise the future of the company. We become hasty sometimes but later we end up realizing hard facts and hence realize that we need to be really soulful with our thoughts", says Umesh.

Like Amity Incubator, most incubators basically bring three things to the table:

- Infrastructure including space and shared services.

- A small amount of funds usually ranging between USD 1 million to USD 10 million. However, recently some of the incubators have even committed as much as half a million dollars.

- A network of Advisors, Investors and Mentors, which help, the entrepreneur to scale and iron out many strategic deficiencies.

Many of the incubators have also started regularly organizing a demo day, where all the entrepreneurs can present to a panel of Investors and try to raise the next round of funding. This has made incubators hot destinations for Investors who can now find quality opportunities to invest in one location.

In this story of Umesh, we thought of having a word from Mr. Ojasvi Babber also, who is the Deputy General Manager of Amity Innovation Incubator and was a mentor to Circuit Sutra, helping it to reach where it has today.

Mr. Ojasvi says:

"We have seen Circuit Sutra grow in terms of Orders and Resource strength over the years. Umesh, the CEO of Circuit Sutra is a person worth mentoring, who acknowledges and appreciates the feedback and suggestions shared with him. His structured approach towards making the transition from a services organization to an IP driven organization gave us conviction in his execution capabilities and his overall vision of the growth of the organization. His articulate Business Presentation and complete transparency of records and documentation made the diligence process easier to go through. The recommendations of Circuit Sutra's work, as received from his customers, strengthened our belief in the team and growth of the organization. All these facts and revelations, along with the growing market demand and unique positioning of the organization, contributed to our decision of investing in Circuit Sutra.

Since Circuit Sutra had been incubated at the Amity Innovation Incubator, It made it a lot easier to interact and understand the processes of the organization and monitor on regular basis the pipeline and the growth. Amity Innovation Incubator was also a regular contributor to the overall strategy of the Organization. Circuit Sutra's receptive and co-operative approach made it easier to understand and align to the objectives of the organization. This also helped us understand the industry and the dynamics better.

We started the exercise of financial consulting Circuit Sutra only when they moved into the incubator. Had the Incubator been involved earlier, it would

have been easier for us to advise Circuit Sutra to structure the fund raising exercise for even the earlier rounds and this would have helped the organization to grow with better focus and less liabilities as against the interim dilution of focus for giving partial exit to the earlier investors"

So while incubation seems to be a great way for an entrepreneur to raise funds, there are some challenges which come along with it.

Since incubation revolves around the entrepreneur working out of the common premises, it may involve having to shift your city for anywhere between three to six months. Also, since most incubators will give you only limited seats, it is not suitable for ideas, which need a large team.

Incubators are not suitable for projects, which have gone beyond the initial stages, as at that time there is usually a requirement of a marketing and a support team. Also, it would be a challenge for such companies to let go of their current team and then rebuild it after the incubation period.

Typically, incubators work best for technology or IP projects where the entrepreneur, along with a couple of other developers, is able to build the product out of the incubator and then shift out to a regular office when he moves onto the sales cycle.

Fund-O- Drama

Funding Technique – **Raise funds from an Incubator**

Prerequisites: Primarily focused on creating a technology product. should be in the early stages of development where only a small team is required.

Time to fund	Less More
Ease of fund	Low High
Amount	Less More

23

Start Up India for a Prosperous India

(Image courtesy: www.narendramodi.in)

#Start Up India is the new motto and the first of its kind initiative by any government. It goes to show that the culture of Entrepreneurship with Innovation, Technology and other peripherals has finally arrived. Until now, one could only dream and discuss one's passions and adrenaline rush to start one's own venture, but only a few could cut across all barriers to turn their dream into reality.

Often, an entrepreneur feared the dictatorship of banks, licenses and the plethora of things which would engulf him and make him lose his vision of achieving milestones. The erratic way of starting a venture in India would primarily dissuade him from even dreaming about doing so.

As per a survey conducted some time ago by a leading portal called www. doingbusiness.org,India ranked 130th for the year 2016 under the category of Ease of Doing Business which was based on various parameters like license, government regulations, finance availability and many more.

The good news is that the ranking has improved tremendously as compared to the rankings earlier to 2016. India ranked a pathetic 186 and hence we can see the effort that must have gone in to ensure the rise upwards. The major credit for this goes to Mr. Narendra Modi who has aptly ensured that we benefit from the culture of Startup India, the New Age India. The effort of the government in power to transform India with #MakeInIndia and #StartUpIndia drives is impeccable.

But many of us would wonder why this initiative is only for India? Is there any logic to it? Will it help us improve anything? The simple answers to the various questions that may pop out of our thought process are growth and development.

India is ranked as one of the top economies in the world which has Youth power. A large chunk of India's population is young, having a high adrenaline rush, is educated and has immense passion and talent to make things happen. Additionally, we have ample resources of every kind which makes us eligible to produce almost anything, supply to the world market and generate good foreign exchange. We are cost-effective, have the power of knowledge, and the determination and grit to make things happen. All this goes to show that India is indeed a Mecca for the much awaited drive, #StartUpIndia.

The very first mention of this revolutionizing drive #StartUpIndia was made on 15th August 2015 by the Honorable PM at Red Fort in his Independence Day speech. He underlined independence from job slavery, which is probably his vision, as he proudly says that he wants to turnaround the youth to be brand ambassadors by being job creators and not job seekers.

The initiative was launched with full aplomb in January 2016 and took the world by storm as it was very much required from a government body and came about at just the right time.

Until then, a lot had happened in the much-talked about Start-up Ecosystem and a plethora of start-up's had set the ball rolling. The ecosystem kept evolving with the on-boarding of many a VC's. Angel investors and institutions were coming ahead in a big way to support the tech-age youth with ample funds to begin their ventures. This was promising and now, with this initiative in place, the ecosystem is only going to be scaling up.

But before we dwell on the movement of start-ups started by the Modi government, let us first understand what and how the movement defines a start-up on their URL www.start-upindia.gov.in-

- Start-up means an entity, incorporated or registered in India not prior to five years, with annual turnover not exceeding 3,571,428 USD in any preceding financial year, working towards innovation, development, deployment or commercialization of new products, processes or services driven by technology or intellectual property.

- Provided that such entity is not formed by splitting up, or reconstruction, of a business already in existence.

- Provided also that an entity shall cease to be a Start-up if its turnover for the previous financial years has exceeded 3,571,428 USD or it has completed 5 years from the date of incorporation/registration.

- Provided further that a Start-up shall be eligible for tax benefits only after it has obtained certification from the Inter-Ministerial Board, setup for such purpose.

Objective of the #StartUpIndia Movement-

To create a single point of contact for the entire Start-up ecosystem and enable knowledge exchange and access to funding.

Details –

Young Indians today have the conviction to venture out on their own and a conducive ecosystem lets them watch their ideas come to life. In today's environment we have more start-ups and entrepreneurs than ever before and the movement is at the cusp of a revolution. However, many start-ups do not reach their full potential due to limited guidance and access.

The Government of India has taken various measures to improve the ease of doing business and is also building an exciting and enabling environment for these start-ups, with the launch of the 'Start-up India' movement.

The 'Start-up India Hub' will be a key stakeholder in this vibrant ecosystem and will:

- Work in a hub and spoke model and collaborate with the Central and State governments, Indian and foreign VCs, angel networks, banks, incubators, legal partners, consultants, universities and R&D institutions.

- Assist start-ups through their lifecycle with specific focus on important aspects like obtaining financing, feasibility testing, business structuring advisory, enhancement of marketing skills, technology commercialization and management evaluation.

- Organize mentorship programs in collaboration with government organizations, incubation centers, educational institutions and private organizations who aspire to foster innovation. To all young Indians who have the courage to enter an environment of risk, the Start-up India Hub will be their friend, mentor and guide to hold their hand and walk with them through this journey.

The key points of #StartUpIndia are-

- Single Window Clearance even with the help of a mobile application

- A unique mobile app which you can download from www.start- upindia. gov.in will enable you to have faster clearances, thus saving crucial time and energy in running around

- 10,000 crore fund of funds to be invested in various Start-ups

- That's a huge kitty to begin with. There could be millions of ideas pertaining to Technology, Innovation and other such USP's highlighted by this initiative, thus making the process more desirable

- 80% reduction in patent registration fee

- Modified and more friendly Bankruptcy Code to ensure 90-day exit window

- Freedom from mystifying inspections for 3 years

- Freedom from Capital Gains Tax for 3 years

- Freedom from tax in profits for 3 years

- Eliminating red tape

- Self-certification compliance

-Through the app, the entrepreneur can get self-certified based on nine Labour and Environment laws which are as follows:

Labour Laws:

- The Building and Other Construction Workers (Regulation of Employment & Conditions of Service) Act, 1996

- The Inter-State Migrant Workmen (Regulation of Employment & Conditions of Service) Act, 1979

- The Payment of Gratuity Act, 1972

- The Contract Labour (Regulation and Abolition) Act, 1970

- The Employees' Provident Funds and Miscellaneous Provisions Act, 1952

- The Employees' State Insurance Act, 1948

Environment Laws:

- The Water (Prevention & Control of Pollution) Act, 1974

- The Water (Prevention & Control of Pollution) Cess (Amendment) Act, 2003

- The Air (Prevention & Control of Pollution) Act, 1981

- Innovation hub under Atal Innovation Mission

- Starting with 5 lakh schools to target 10 lakh children for innovation programme

- New schemes to provide IPR protection to start-ups and new firms

- Encourage entrepreneurship

- Position India across the world as a start-up hub

These are the broader levels or the over-the-surface highlights and key deliverables. There would be many which shall also become the key points of the initiative. For instance, employment creation, foreign exchange benefits to the country, advance technology encouragement and many more such benefits would be visible.

Shri Narendra Modi had quoted, "I see start-ups, technology and innovation as exciting and effective instruments for India's transformation."

Yes indeed! Start-ups can very well transform the country as they can bring Innovation, Technology, Talent, ample resources and much more for everyone to benefit from.

The Action Plan booklet/guide launched under the #StartupIndia Initiative lists down the various steps and explains the entire process very diligently. The same is also available online on the portal www.start-upindia.gov.in

Going further on the Action Plan and in order to meet the objectives of the initiative, the Government of India is announcing this Action Plan that addresses all aspects of the Start-up ecosystem.

With this Action Plan, the Government hopes to accelerate the spreading of the Start-up movement:

- From digital/technology sector to a wide array of sectors including agriculture, manufacturing, social sector, healthcare, education etc., and

- From existing tier 1 cities to tier 2 and tier 3 cities including semi-urban and rural areas. The Action Plan is divided across the following areas:

  (i) Simplification and Handholding

  (ii) Funding Support and Incentives

  (iii) Industry-Academia Partnership and Incubation

The government created URL www.start-upindia.gov.in specifies every aspect on how could one benefit from the initiative.

The portal of Start-up India promises everything. Right from policies to funds, an entrepreneur can manage everything. There is a list of SEBI (Securities and Exchange Board of India) authorised incubators and registered funds which means that once the start-up can prove that it can deliver, it will surely be funded. An entrepreneur needs to submit any one of the following documents.

But before you start to jump with joy, please note a very important aspect of this drive.

A start-up to you is once you have begun with the bare minimum and necessary resources, but for the #StartUpIndia scheme, it is essential to qualify as a Start-up in ANY ONE of the following:

a) Recommendation (with regard to innovative nature of business), in a format specified by Department of Industrial Policy and Promotion, from any Incubator established in a post-graduate college in India; or

b) Letter of support by any Incubator which is funded (in relation to the project) from Government of India or any State Government as part of any specified scheme to promote innovation; or

c) Recommendation (with regard to innovative nature of business), in a format specified by Department of Industrial Policy and Promotion, from any Incubator recognized by Government of India; or

d) Letter of funding of not less than 20 percent in equity by any Incubation Fund/ Angel Fund/ Private Equity Fund/ Accelerator/ Angel Network duly registered with Securities and Exchange Board of India that endorses innovative nature of the business. Department of Industrial Policy and Promotion may include any such fund in a negative list for such reasons as it may deem fit; or

e) Letter of funding by Government of India or any State Government as part of any specified scheme to promote innovation; or

f) Patent filed and published in the Journal by the India Patent Office in areas affiliated with the nature of business being promoted.

Any one of the above documents is necessary to get yourself recognized as a start- up. Once you are recognized as a start-up in the #StartupIndia scheme, you can avail various benefits of the taxes and other things under it.

Now the next obvious query for any wannabe entrepreneur would be, "I can do this as I have the vision of being an entrepreneur but I do not know how to structure myself to achieve my vision."

Not to worry as #StartupIndia has taken care of this as well. The scheme has launched the Atal Innovation Mission (AIM) with Self-Employment and Talent Utilization (SETU) Program.

The objective of doing this was:

To serve as a platform for promotion of world-class Innovation Hubs, Grand Challenges, Start-up businesses and other self-employment activities, particularly in technology driven areas.

The Atal Innovation Mission (AIM) shall have two core functions:

- Entrepreneurship promotion through Self-Employment and Talent Utilization (SETU), wherein innovators would be supported and mentored to become successful entrepreneurs

- Innovation promotion: to provide a platform where innovative ideas are generated

The main components proposed to be undertaken as part of the mission include:

- Establishment of sector specific Incubators including in PPP mode (refer number 14 of this Action Plan under the URL given on www.start- upindia. gov.in).

- Establishment of 500 Tinkering Labs.

- Pre-incubation training to potential entrepreneurs in various technology areas in collaboration with various academic institutions having expertise in the field.

- Strengthening of incubation facilities in existing incubators and mentoring of Start-ups.

- Seed funding to potentially successful and high growth Start-ups Innovation promotion.

- Institution of Innovation Awards (3 per state/UT) and 3 National level awards.

- Providing support to State Innovation Councils for awareness creation and organizing state level workshops/conferences.

- Launch of Grand Innovation Challenge Awards for finding ultra-low cost solutions to India's pressing and intractable problems.

Therefore, we can see that a lot of thinking has gone into designing the new age India model which shall help transform India to be an India which we all have always wanted - a Superpower!

This initiative shall certainly help the youth to achieve this dream for themselves and for the country. #StartUpIndia will certainly live upto the literal meaning of its name and that is Starting India to a new league to outshine others and emerge a booming economy.

The Action Plan on the portal mentions everything about every step that you probably need to take to get your actions right and to fulfil your much-awaited dream.

C'mon India! Welcome a new beginning and become the new age #StartUpIndia.

Raising Funds: Legal Perspective

Contributed by

Nidhish Mehrotra ANM Global Inc (Leading Advisor to
Fortune 500 Global Companies, SME's and Startups)

Launching a new business or expanding an existing business set-up requires capital. Raising capital from various sources is an indispensable step to commence or expand a business. Expansion of a business is financed either by internal cash flows or concerted capital raising efforts from angel investors, venture capital investors or other private equity investors.

From the legal perspective, it has to be made sure by the founders of a business that all essential legal compliances and filings have been completed. This is because investors desire to have the investee company fully compliant with all the legal obligations, so as to avoid any future liabilities.

Prior to investing in a new or existing business venture, investors take a series of steps. Below are the legal aspects to be kept in mind in the investment process:

- Approaching investors: At the very outset, in respect of the first stage of the 'pitch' and presentation of the business proposal, it is imperative for the promoter to enter into a Non-Disclosure Agreement (NDA) with the investor to ensure that the business proposal/model and the other related details are not disclosed to any third party.

- Term sheets – Term-sheet is a non-binding agreement, which lays down the basic terms and conditions under which an investment is to be made. Basically, it serves as a template to draft further detailed legal documents. Once the parties reach an agreement with respect to the provisions elucidated in the term sheet, a binding agreement or contract is drawn up in accordance with the term sheet details.

- Due Diligence (financial, legal, labour, tax etc.) by the investor– Due diligence of all material records of the company such as auditor's reports, annual returns, filings with the Registrar of Companies (ROC), licenses and permits, Registration Certificates pertaining to the company's Intellectual Property (IP), Articles of Association, Resolutions, agreements of the company with third parties, agreements with the promoter and his relatives /associate companies, any supply agreements and all other material contracts. After the due diligence is done, the investors require the details regarding the necessary deficient legal compliances, which have to be rectified as a pre-condition before signing and executing the final agreements.

- Structuring Investment Instruments: Equity, Debt, Hybrid –

   (i) Equity means investment in exchange for issue/transfer of shares of the investee company. The return for an equity share is in the form of dividend. Additionally, equity shares entitle the shareholder to certain voting rights with respect to the affairs of the company. Depending upon the investment, investors may want to play a role in the operations of the company and hence, utilize the voting rights. Sometimes, investors may require the investee company to give them extensive voting rights like veto rights mandating that the investee company cannot make certain decisions without the permission of the investors.

   (ii) Debt instruments do not entitle any ownership in the company. It may be in the form of conditional loan or debentures. A conditional loan is generally repayable in the form of royalty after the venture is able to generate sales. It may also be subject to interest payable at fixed or variable rate. Debentures are loan instruments and are not part of the share capital of a company. Essentially, a debenture is a loan capital and the issuing company is liable to pay interest thereon, whether there are profits or not.

   (iii) Hybrid – Instruments in the form of preference shares, convertible debentures or convertible preference shares are termed as "hybrid". A preference shareholder does not get any voting rights in the company but gets a preference over the other shareholders in respect of dividend. Convertible Instruments (whether debentures or preference shares) get converted into equity shares based on a specified conversion ratio, upon maturity. Till the time of conversion, they would continue to get dividend/interest at the specified rate. However, a convertible instrument will carry no voting rights till the time of conversion. These may be converted depending upon the terms and conditions of the issue. Further, investors generally provide for conversion in case of continuous failure by the investee company to pay dividend/interest.

- Definitive Agreements: Investment Agreement, Shareholder's Agreement (SHA) – The Investment Agreement is signed to elucidate the key terms & conditions, rights and liabilities and indemnities of the parties involved, during the investment process and subsequently. The SHA contains key rights over the shares issued to the investor, governance provisions of the investee company (like appointment/removal of

The Startup Ecosystem

The Startup Ecosystem

Contributed by
Vishwas Mahajan, President-TiE Pune

Chapter (TiE-The Indus Entrepreneurs)

The Role of the Ecosystem

Ecosystem is a word that is often used in the whole entrepreneurship paradigm

and this is a word that has been borrowed from biology in fact.

An ecosystem basically implies that several parts or several members or components of a living system actually help each other and collaborate so that the whole system survives and grows.

In the entrepreneurial ecosystem, we can equate these to investors, services providers like lawyers and accountants, customers, technology validators, incubators, Venture Capitalists, mentors and advisors, the regulatory ecosystem, the risk management ecosystems and so on.

If an entrepreneur has to succeed, it is actually vital for these ecosystem components to work largely in favor of the entrepreneur.

If that does not happen, this proportionate amount of time and financial investments are made to mitigate some of these issues, which then jeopardize the viability of an enterprise.

The ecosystem in fact benefits from the other members of the ecosystem performing and doing their duties and providing a supportive environment because the success of one of the components ensures that the entire system will be successful.

It is in this context that looking at the Indian perspective we need to do a lot of work in a supportive ecosystem that helps an entrepreneur at every step of the way.

The Role of TiE

TiE being an, of the entrepreneurs, for the entrepreneurs, by the entrepreneurs kind of organization, is in a pivotal position to provide the kind of ecosystem support that an entrepreneur needs at the start of his or her own journey.

TiE itself, with its philosophy of creating a self-fulfilling cycle of wealth creation by promoting and supporting entrepreneurs, is in fact the ideal vehicle to connect all the other pieces together. Whether it is investors, advisors, incubators or it is mentors, customers and the like, TiE has no vested interest other than the success of an entrepreneur. The role of TiE is to connect all these pieces of the puzzle together and become a glue so that the entrepreneur can rely on TiE as its own ally rather than an entity that needs to get business or get something from him or her. In some of the ecosystems that I have seen in India, the other ecosystem players involve people who are in the business advocacy or lobbying type of activities. The chambers of commerce, CII and FICCIs of the world will be a part of this category.

There are geographical entities that provide impetus for specific geography promotion. So, there is Japan, Germany, UK and sometimes there are other states to promote investments in their regions.

There are funding folks - either angel groups or VC's. There are the customer organizations like Retailers association of India, Indian banking federation or the like. There are technology enablers like Amazon web services. There are large corporates that operate incubator services and find startups like Microsoft and SAPs of the world.

All these and more have their own agendas, which, while it is supportive to the entrepreneur's interest, is not exclusively for the interest of the entrepreneur.

Here TiE can play a major role because the only interest TiE has is in the wellbeing and success of an entrepreneur because it works in this space. TiE also becomes a go-to organization for these organizations to access the networks and collaborate with TiE, which in turn helps entrepreneurs to access these resources through TiE. So it is a win-win combination in enabling entrepreneurs to succeed.

There are several programs that TiE carries out and, being a global organization, one of the things I am most excited about is its global connectivity. Global connectivity means if an entrepreneur in one region needs to access resources from other regions of the world, the opportunity exists to use TiE to do that.

In addition to the regular programs, TiE has a role to play in each of the important thing like inspiration, networking and educating the entrepreneurs.

Entrepreneurship is a lonely journey and you need people who are your peers.

Some of my story sessions and activities that are done are to connect and hear about what other people are doing, which is a great source of great inspiration.

The networking opportunities that TiE can offer are limitless. An entrepreneur needs basic skills and knowledge and at many times, at appropriate stages of business, these become vital.

It is TiE's role to provide those inputs to entrepreneurs at the appropriate stage whether it is financial, technology or marketing or any of the things that are needed.

So, in my opinion, an organization like TiE, which has a selfless interest in promoting entrepreneurs is critical for the entrepreneurship ecosystem.

Startups and Funding Perspective

When I am in a room with a few startups and I question them on what is that one thing that is keeping them from achieving their entrepreneurial goals, invariably I get funding as an answer.

However, when I dig a little bit deeper, I find this may not be the case because even assuming, the startup got funding, the question whether that would be the solutions for all the issues he or she has is unclear. Many times one sees funding as an easy need but there are several things that an entrepreneur needs to look at. There is a whole product market fit, there is a whole business model validation. There is an issue with customer development and pivoting the basic concept, then there is technology, the scalability, the ease of use of your products, your team and several such things. Many of these things that I have listed are actually within the control of the entrepreneur to explore and execute and validate.

Several times you see entrepreneurs getting engrossed in the original idea that he or she has and starting to look for funding without doing some of the basic diligence on the idea and some of the components that I have listed. It is always said that the best person or the best organization to fund the startup is a customer. If there is someone that is willing to pay for the idea or the product that the entrepreneur is developing, that is, first of all, the biggest validation and secondly, this customer does not want equity and provides a great reference. So, to me, the top most priority for funding for an entrepreneur should be to get funded by a customer. There are several examples of this happening.

In order for you to be funded by the customer without going out of pocket, the whole concept of lean startups comes in wherein we are trying to develop an idea with least efforts and earliest validation from the customers. Unless the project that the entrepreneur is embarking on has a high capital outlay and upfront costs without which the project simply cannot go forward, the need for very high upfront investment can be mitigated by working smartly and getting your early customers to fund the idea.

The second best funding alternative is your own savings and investments and/or your friends and family.

Now here there is a great opportunity for us to convince our near and dear ones about the idea and have them put money where their mouth is. On the flip side, if they are not able to convince the people that have known him or her for a long time, there is very little chance that they will be able to convince the outsiders to do so. Essentially people are funded by those who believe in them and so establishing the credibility to your friends and family about your idea is a good starting point.

Mostly when you say funding, it is synonymous with seed funding or angel investing or Venture Capital's various rounds. Now, I would say that in order to seek outside funding, several steps that have to be done internally by the entrepreneur need to be taken care of. However, it is a very significant milestone for an entrepreneur to get funded from an institutional or an outside investor. It not only provides the validation from the scalability perspective where an investor thinks that the concept can scale and provide the returns that is anticipated, but without this the, investment will not come.

So, when you go for an investment opportunity, the entrepreneur must keep in mind that some of the initial steps have been taken care of and the concept is scalable enough for an outside investor to invest, given that there is a fair amount of risk that the maturity of an investment that an investor makes will actually not yield the results.

So my only advice will be to go for outside finding when you are ready with some of the things that we discussed earlier. Remember that going for funding and pitching to investors can take a lot of bandwidth and time. This is the exact amount of time that you may require for working on your early customers or building the product or other activities.

Given that the time the entrepreneur has is finite, the prioritization of where that time should be spent becomes important and if it is just one co-founder or one or two co-founder kind of situation, the amount of time required and the investment of time needed for securing funding can actually be detrimental to some other critical aspects of building the business. Many times if it is a larger co-founding team and if the team has defined the roles and responsibilities, it is a good idea for one of the co-founders to dedicate him or her primarily for the job of finding funding and going through the whole process. This way the other activities that are critical to business continue to happen and the effort required for funding can also in parallel be continued with one of the cofounders.

I am not going to actually discuss the details of business planning and market validation and other things as I am sure this will be covered in other parts of the book.

TiE Pune has been in the forefront of nurturing startups and entrepreneurs. Some of the programs that I have talked about earlier have created a vibrant community which is connected through TiE. In addition to the activities that I have listed above, one of the programs that we are most excited about is our nurturing initiative where typically, at the beginning of the year, startups are invited to join the program wherein an established senior entrepreneur becomes a part of the core team of a startup to help guide the startup to the next phase.

The significant time and emotional commitment that a mentor makes in the business of the startup makes a difference and we have seen some significant results of that! We are into the 3rd round of this and with every round, the nurtured program has only improved. Enthusiastic mentors provide not only the mentorship, but also their vital connections and even funding, although these are not part of the mentoring initiative.

Many of the organizations that have gone through the nurturing initiatives have achieved success in organizing their business in a better way, scaling it, getting funding. One such example is an organization named Altizon, where I heard that in the most recent round of nurture, they have signed a term sheet for funding, which will happen in 2 rounds, one immediately and then a follow up round a year from now.

We are really excited about some of the successes that our nurtured mentees have scored and this allows us to dedicate ourselves in making this program more proactive and result oriented.

Printed in the United States
By Bookmasters